Books by Wright Morris

Novels

Plains Song

The Fork River Space Project

A Life

War Games

Fire Sermon

In Orbit

One Day

Cause for Wonder

What a Way to Go

Ceremony in Lone Tree

Love Among the Cannibals

The Field of Vision

The Huge Season

The Deep Sleep

The Works of Love

Man and Boy

The World in the Attic

The Man Who Was There

My Uncle Dudley

Photo-Text

Love Affair: A Venetian Journal

God's Country and My People

The Home Place

The Inhabitants

Essays

Earthly Delights, Unearthly Adornments

About Fiction

A Bill of Rites, A Bill of Wrongs, A Bill of Goods

The Territory Ahead

Anthology

Wright Morris: A Reader

Short Stories

Real Losses, Imaginary Gains

Memoirs

Will's Boy

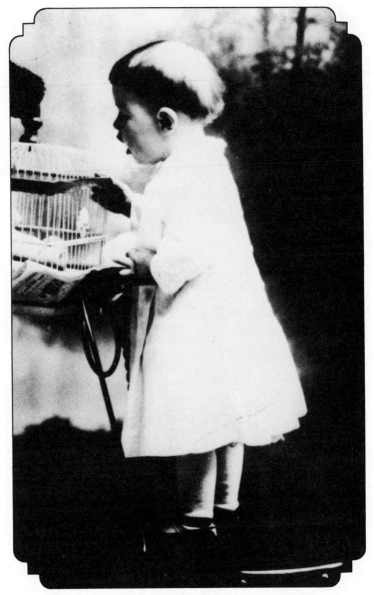

Will's Boy

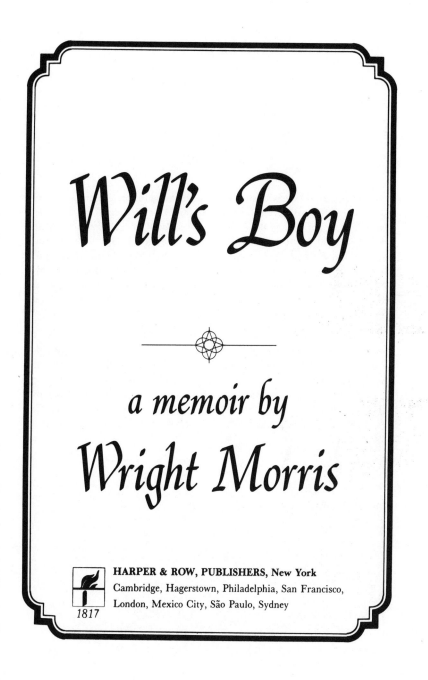

Will's Boy

a memoir by
Wright Morris

HARPER & ROW, PUBLISHERS, New York
Cambridge, Hagerstown, Philadelphia, San Francisco,
London, Mexico City, São Paulo, Sydney

1817

Grateful acknowledgment is made to the following for permission to reprint. University of Nebraska Press Bison Books editions for selections from *My Uncle Dudley,* copyright 1942 by Wright Morris; *The Man Who Was There,* copyright 1945 by Wright Morris; *The Works of Love,* copyright 1949, 1951 by Wright Morris; *The Field of Vision,* copyright © 1956 by Wright Morris; *Cause for Wonder,* copyright © 1963 by Wright Morris; *One Day,* copyright © 1965 by Wright Morris; Charles Scribner's Sons for selections from *The Inhabitants,* copyright 1946 by Wright Morris; Harper & Row, Publishers, Inc. for selections from *Real Losses, Imaginary Gains,* copyright © 1976 by Wright Morris; *Earthly Delights, Unearthly Adornments,* copyright © 1978 by Wright Morris.

FIRST EDITION

Designer: Robin Malkin

Library of Congress Cataloging in Publication Data

Morris, Wright, 1910–
   Will's boy.
   1. Morris, Wright, 1910–   —Biography—Youth.
   2. Novelists, American—20th century—Biography.
   I. Title.
PS3525.07475Z476   1981   813'.52 [B]   80-8708
ISBN 0-06-014856-X   AACR2

---

81 82 83 84 85 10 9 8 7 6 5 4 3 2 1

For Buz Wyeth

To the Reader

*F*ew things are so wondrous as our assurance that we are each at the center of a cosmos. Nor does learning we are not long disturb us. In the early thralldom of this feeling we accumulate the indelible impressions we will ceaselessly ponder but never question, pebbles that we fondle in the mind's secret pockets. One center and one only lies within us, as clearly perceived in a dream of Joseph, told by Thomas Mann.

> *For lo, the world hath many centers,*
> *one for each created being, and about*
> *each one it lieth in its own circle.*

Since first reading those words my mind has sought an image that is commensurate with my wonder. One I find congenial is that of a vast tranquil pond on which a light rain is falling. Each drop that falls is the center of a circle that is soon overlapped by other circles. The apparent obliteration of the circle does not eliminate the radiating vibrations. This image of endlessly renewed and expanding circles is my own ponderable cosmos.

The first of my childhood impressions is that of lampglow and shadows on a low ceiling. But under my steadfast gaze it dissolves like tissue. It resists both fixing and enlargement. What I am left with is the ache of a nameless longing. On my child's soul lampglow and shadows have left radiating circles that a lifetime drizzle, of lapping and overlapping, have not washed away.

I was born on the sixth of January, 1910, in the Platte
Valley of Nebraska, just south of the 41st parallel,
just west of the 98th meridian, just to the north, or south,
or a bit to the east of where it sometimes rained, but more
than likely it didn't, less than a mile from what had once
been the Lone Tree station of the Pony Express on the
Overland Trail.

My father had come west from Ohio to begin a new
life with the Union Pacific Railroad in Chapman, Nebraska. My mother had been born on the bluffs south of
the Platte in a house with the cupola facing the view to
the west. They met in the barber shop of Eddie Cahow,
who had come up from Texas on the Chisholm Trail, but
found that he preferred barbering to a life in the saddle.
The open range had been closed by strips of barbed wire,

3

and the plow, for both better and worse, had replaced the six-shooter and the man on horseback, a change predicted when the town called Lone Tree at its founding was changed to Central City before I was born. Early settlers felt, and with reason, that a Lone Tree might encourage maverick, wandering males, but discourage most marriageable females. My childhood impressions were not of the big sky, and the endless vistas, but of the blaze of light where the trees ended, the sheltered grove from where I peered at the wagons of the gypsies camped at its edge.

Six days after my birth my mother died. Having stated this bald fact, I ponder its meaning. In the wings of my mind I hear voices, I am attentive to the presence of invisible relations, I see the ghosts of people without faces. Almost twenty years will pass before I set knowing eyes on my mother's people. Her father, a farmer and preacher of the Seventh-Day Adventist gospel, shortly after her death would gather up his family and move to a new Adventist settlement near Boise, Idaho. My life begins, and will have its ending, in this abiding chronicle of real losses and imaginary gains.

My father, William Henry Morris, born on a farm near Zanesville, Ohio, was one of fourteen children, all of whom grew to maturity. In the early 1890s, with his older brother, Harry, he came west to the treeless plains of Nebraska. To my knowledge no one ever referred to my father as Bill. Both friends and relations called him Will. The housekeeper, Anna, brought up from Aurora to take care of a house, a widower, and a motherless child, pronounced this word as in whippoorwilllll, the sound tailing off like the bird's song, greatly enhancing my impression of the man who often took his meals with his hat on. He was a busy father; the bicycle he rode to and from his work often lay on its side, the front wheel still spinning.

On weekends in Chapman the farmers parked their buggies at the hitch bar in front of Cahow's barber shop. This provided free bleacher seat views, for those in the buggies, of the man being clipped or shaved in the chair. If the chair was pumped up, and the occupant erect rather than horizontal, he was able to exchange glances with those peering over the half curtain. In this manner, according to Eddie Cahow, my father first set eyes on my mother, leaping from the chair, the cloth dangling from his collar, to help her down from the buggy. That is the story, and who am I to change it? She was the youngest, and most favored, of the four Osborn girls. Her name was Grace. Her sisters, Winona, Violet and Marion. Grace Osborn and Will Morris were soon married, and used his recently acquired railroad pass to spend their honeymoon in San Francisco, from where he wired the bank to send him another fifty dollars. A son, Fayette Mitchell, born in 1904, lived for only a few days. Six years will pass before I am born, and a few days later Grace Osborn Morris is dead, having given her life that I might live.

On her death a debate arose as to who should raise me, my father or my mother's married sister, Violet. More than sixty years later my Aunt Winona wrote me:

When your mother died my sister Violet wanted to take you, but your father would not consent to it. He said, "He is all I have left of Grace." O dear boy, you were the center of so much suffering, so many losses you will never realize, know or feel . . .

This decision would be crucial to the child who played no part in it. Much of my life would be spent in an effort to recover the losses I never knew, realized or felt, the past that shaped yet continued to elude me. Had Grace Osborn lived, my compass would have been set on a different course, and my sails full of more than the winds of fiction. Am I to register that as a child's loss, or a man's gain?

The small creatures of this world, and not a few of the large ones, are only at their ease under something. The cat crawls under the culvert, the infant under the table, screened off by the cloth that hangs like a curtain . . . in the Platte Valley of Nebraska, street culverts, piano boxes, the seats of wagons and buggies, railroad trestles, low bridges, the dark caves under front porches were all favored places of concealment. With Br'er Fox I shared the instinct to lie low. Seated in dust as fine as talcum, my lap and hands overlaid with a pattern of shadows, I peered out at the world through the holes between the slats.*

In a room of lampglow, where the shadows waver on a low ceiling, I lie full of longing at the side of a woman whose bosom heaves, but she is faceless. Would this be my father's second wife, in a marriage soon ended? Not knowing the nature of the longing I felt, would it persist and reappear as a poignant yearning for what it is in the past that eludes me?

I have another memory of lampglow and shadow. A

**Earthly Delights, Unearthly Adornments*, 1978.

figure looms above me, swaying like smoke, and against the flickering lamplight I see her fingers unbraid her hair. I hear the lisp of the comb, and the rasp of the brush. This will prove to be Anna, a friend of my mother's sisters, who has been hired to take care of me. Heavily, her arms resting on the bed, she kneels to pray. Her hushed whispering voice fills me with awe. To test the height of the wick's flame she stretches one of her gray hairs across the top of the chimney. Did I see it glow, like the filament of a light bulb, or is that something I have imagined, a luminous fiber in my mind, rather than the lamp? My child's soul is enlarged by this nightly ceremony of light and shadow, and the voice of prayer. It is appropriate to this emotion that the details are vague. Later, gripping her hand in the church pew, I feel the throb of her voice before I hear it, and share her passion with fear and trembling.

One reason I see it all so clearly is that I have so often put it into writing. Perhaps it is the writing I remember, the vibrant image I have made of the memory impression. A memory for just such details is thought to be characteristic of the writer, but the fiction is already at work in what he remembers. No deception is intended, but he wants to see clearly what is invariably, intrinsically vague. So he imagines. Image-making is indivisibly a part of remembering.*

In this same house, in my sleepers with the "feet," I hurry to stand on the hot-air floor radiator while I am dressed. In the kitchen my eyes are below the level of the table where raw sugar cookies are being rolled for bak-

Earthly Delights, Unearthly Adornments.

7

ing. I reach and clutch some of the dough: I love its sweet, raw taste.

In the large room at the front, where I lie with pneumonia, the panels of colored glass in the window make a bright pattern on the bedclothes. With my warm breath, and the sleeve of my elbow, I rub a hole in the frosted window and peer out. The world is white. I am able to see the white birches in the yard against the black, twisted buggy lanes in the road. Gifts are placed on the bed. The flames of candles glitter on the Christmas tree tinsel. A huge bearlike man, with a booming voice, comes in with the winter trapped in his coat. He is Dr. Brown. I am puzzled why the fur of his coat is on the inside. For reasons that are not clear he comes to see me only when I am sick.

If I attempt to distinguish between fiction and memory, and press my nose to memory's glass to see more clearly, the remembered image grows more illusive, like the details in a Pointillist painting. I recognize *it, more than I see it. This recognition is a fabric of emotion as immaterial as music. In this defect of memory do we have the emergence of imagination? . . . Precisely where memory is frail and emotion is strong, imagination takes fire.**

Mr. and Mrs. Riddlemosher live in the house on the corner, facing the railroad tracks. It sits flat on the ground. Spears of grass grow between the loose boards on the front porch. In the barrel under the rain spout bugs skitter on the water and polliwogs cast shadows on the

Earthly Delights, Unearthly Adornments.

slimy bottom. The white hairs of a mare's tail, put into the barrel, will turn to garter snakes.

I sit on the side porch of the house building an airplane with rubber bands and matches. Mrs. Riddlemosher, wearing a sunbonnet, picks gooseberries in her garden. The tinfoil I collect from gum and candy wrappers I sell to Mr. Riddlemosher for seven cents a pound. In the summer dusk, from the dark of the alley, I watch my father in the porch off the kitchen crumble cornbread into a tall glass, pour Carnation milk from a can on it, and squish it up and down with the handle of his spoon before he eats it.

I see my father, against the wind-rocked streetlight, standing in his underwear at the open front window. Bells are ringing, whistles are blowing. My father scratches himself as he listens. Thinking it must be the end of the world, I wait for it to end.

I am given a drum for Christmas, and I am aware as I beat it of the power that it gives me to annoy others.

At school I sit in a circle of chairs with my classmates. When my turn comes I go to the blackboard and spell out a word that is my name. I write this word on a piece of lined paper and bring it home—a gift of myself to Anna, who is full of praise. Although largely unobserved, I instinctively take shelter beneath a buggy, a culvert, a porch or a table, from where I peer out.

When did I thieve and strike a box of kitchen matches, sucking the charcoal tips for the flavor of the sulphur? I hear the abrasive scratch of the match, but it does not light up the darkness around me.

Gerald Cole and Dean Cole are my friends. Dean Cole

is small and thin-faced, like a witch, but Gerald Cole is big and round-faced, like a pumpkin, or Happy Hooligan without a can on his head. We run shrieking across the pasture to where the airplane that has done the loop-the-loops limps along like a crippled bird.

So much for my impressions of my friends—what of theirs of me? Was I a sniveler, a tattletale, a crybaby? A snot-nosed little fart, or a slack-jawed snorfler? In all my childhood no mirror or window returns a reflection I remember.

Is it a fact that Gerald Cole, with my collaboration, dipped my head into a barrel of soft roofing tar, then clipped the curls from my head with his father's sheep shears? That is written somewhere. Is it the writing I remember? Sixty-five years later, in a photograph of children gathered in the open for their picture, I recognize myself as the plump-faced open-mouthed child with the adenoids in the first row. My scalp gleams where my hair is parted. On my right, surely, is the witch-faced, apprehensive Dean Cole, wetting his pants. On my left, a bow in her hair, the girl who hid the eggs in our yard at Easter. Not a child in this assembly smiles at the birdie. We are sober, worried, expectant and fearful. Such incidents as I remember are uniformly free of the impression, if any, I made on my companions. I am a camera, but who it is that clicks the shutter I do not know.

The long, long thoughts of childhood approximate dreaming in the way they hover between waking and sleeping. The voice the child attends to is the one that speaks without the need of an answer—the voice of fire, of thunder, of wind, rain and silence.

If I had had faculties of a different order—what my

father would have called the brains I was born with—the changing pitch of the mail train's whistle as it approached from the west, then receded, would have given my dreaming mind something to ponder, but I preferred the shimmering fragment of suspended time that I saw through the porch slats where the train had just been, but was no more.

Neither the bitter cold of winter, nor the heat of summer, nor rolling balls of fire caused by lightning, nor straw driven through the planks of a barn left on me the indelible impression of a fuzzless caterpillar, green as quicklime and spotted with bull's-eyes, seen in the fresh manure in the dark of the stable. Nor did my father's horse, his tail sweeping the buckboard, lead me to marvel as I did at the time seen on my new dollar watch. The even tenor of this time was occasionally broken by the spring Chautauqua, in the weeds behind the water tower, or the Hagenbeck and Wallace circus, the train pulled on the siding beyond the cattle loader where the caged animals howled at the edge of darkness. Found weeping at the carnival, where I had lost fifteen cents in the sawdust, the voice that comforted me said, "You're Will's boy, aren't you?" And so I proved to be.

My memory of the caterpillar is still green as money, but I see nothing whatsoever of the food on my plate, if my feet are shod or bare, if my face is freckled, if my nose is runny, if I wear knee-length britches or bulging rompers, or if the glass ball on the doily on the sewing machine snows like a winter blizzard when it is shaken.

She would come up with her lamp, the wick swimming in oil, and cross the room like the figures in his dreams, *without taking steps. Holding the lamp close to his face, she would see that he was asleep. He would feel the heat of the lamp on his forehead, catch a whiff of the oil. She would first open the damper, then turn with the lamp so that the room darkened behind her, but her snow white hair seemed to trap the light. During the day it would be piled high on her head, but when she came up with the lamp it would be in braids. With a silver handled comb that rattled when she used it, she would comb out the tangled ends of the braids. Out would come, like the burrs in a dog's tail, the knotted hairs. When all the hairs stood up straight, like a brush, she would pass the ends over the flame in the chimney, where they would curl at the tips and crackle with a frying sound. The smell was like that when she singed a chicken over a hole in the kitchen range, turning the bird slowly in the flame of a cob dipped in kerosene.**

On Hallowe'en, big, rough, loud-mouthed boys came out of hiding and carted privies into the square on flat farm wagons. On the one with the cushioned seats I read the words NO MAN'S LAND, the wickedness of which did not escape me.

I sang and whistled "Over There" and "It's a Long Way to Tipperary" without concern as to where it was.

A movie, *The Beast of Berlin,* was shown at Donaldson's theater, to which I gained admission by distributing leaflets. When the Kaiser Devil appeared on the silver screen we pelted him with tomatoes and rotten eggs.

In the lot beside the tracks, where the cow was pas-

* The Field of Vision, 1956.

tured, boxes and cartons were piled as high as the telephone wires, on top of which a scarecrow figure with a funnel hat was thrown to be burned. In this way the Kaiser Devil was burned in effigy. When the fire cooled, Gerald Cole and I retrieved the blackened funnel and returned it to his mother.

I was cautioned not to bother my father at his work in the station, or risk being killed by crossing the tracks. In the long summer dusk, if I looked to the east, I might see the smoking fires of hoboes behind the piles of track ties, or the covered wagons of the gypsies near the switch tower, their hobbled horses munching the ditch grass. To the west, if the lights were on, I would see my father's pale face, green in the shadow cast by his visor. If the window stood open I might hear the cricket chirp of the telegraph key. The light would glitter on the metal strips for sealing freight cars, hanging like keys from a loop of wire, or the polished knobs of the rubber stamps that had to be stamped to be read. If I waited long enough I would see the semaphore, west of the cattle loader, switch from red to green.

The summer I was old enough to roller skate, a short stretch of concrete paving was put into the street just behind the depot. What shift in continental gravity dictated that when this piece of paving was extended it would go to the east, not to the west? I reflected this same shift in allegiance in my preference, on the station platform, for the wide diner windows of the eastbound trains when they stopped for water. From the platform I observed the white-jacketed, black-faced porters pour water into the gleaming crystal glasses. I exchanged glances with smiling faces. I cared little about where these people were from, but I was captivated by where they were going. On the map on the wall in the station lobby all of the railroad lines converged on Chicago, the home of Montgomery Ward and Sears and Roebuck. It did not interest me that some lines continued to other places. Chicago was where the trains went and the roads ended. I do not recall hearing my father speak of a place called New York.

Once it had entered town from the east, the Lincoln Highway made a dog-leg turn at the "square," an open space where five streets converged, in order that the main street would exit parallel to the Union Pacific Railroad as it followed the curve of the Platte Valley. This confusion of streets impinging on the square left me both perplexed and enlarged. I was living not in one town only, but two towns, each of which had its own railroad. The Burlington, that came up from Aurora one day, and went down to it several days later, had a locomotive with a funnel-shaped smokestack and a cowcatcher that actually caught cows. On the brick station platform where it came to a stop the pistons hissed warm steam on my bare feet and legs. Down this track to the south, on a rusty spur, was the sandpit rumored to be bottomless with sinks of quicksand at its edges. From the raft on its surface I could peer into its depths, or gaze at the shimmering foreshortened image of myself. On one occasion, with Anna, I had traveled to Aurora with butterflies that flew in and out of the coach windows. Where these tracks crossed the Union Pacific a switch tower had been erected, square as a blockhouse, with the windows at the top so wide I could watch the man in the tower seize and grapple with the switch levers. If there were freight cars on the spur to the cattle loader I might climb to the top of the cars to munch my nut Hershey, or chew the whips of licorice and spit juice on the rails. I was never long free—once I was conscious of it—of my impression of time as a liquid in which all things were suspended, a space measured by the flights of sparrows and pigeons.

One Sunday I am driven, by horse and buggy, past the cemetery where my mother lies buried. A man with a scythe cut the grass between the stones. I was saddened but comforted by the thought that my mother, in heaven, had her eyes on me.

In a room flooded with light I lie on a table and have my adenoids out. Afterward, to quench my thirst, I am given bottles of grape juice and put in the rear of the buggy where I can whoop it up. After whooping it up, I can drink more of it. Down the road the sun smokes, the sky blazes with light that spreads on the plain, splashing on objects. It shames me to know that my mother's eyes are on me, my own burning with tears.

Through the vines was Bickel's General Store and a brown dog drinking at the fountain. Sparrows dropped from the trees to the wires and then from the wires to the ditch grass. A pigeon dropped from the belfry to the roof of the barn. He went along the tin roof to the hole, dropped inside. Jewel's Tea Wagon passed and the dust came up and went by. More sparrows dropped from the wires, stirred the grass near the road. Mrs. Riddlemosher stopped picking currants and turned with her pan. Mrs. Willard came and stood at the screen. Behind the feed

15

store Mr. Cole's mare whinnied and Mr. Bickel smoothed
his apron, stopped shooing flies. Tipping her sunbonnet
back, Mrs. Riddlemosher looked toward the square where
*the dust came marching down the road with the rain.**

Clearly, from a low point of elevation, I see the street, with its crisp afternoon shadows, the corner where the main street dog-legs to the left, the barber shop and its pole, the blazing window of the hardware store, the fringe-topped buggy held up at the crossing gates until the eastbound flier thunders past. Few images, after more than sixty years, are more indelible. What explains it? I was seated in Dr. Brown's office on a high wire-handled potty, waiting for the final verdict in my long battle with a tapeworm.

An hour or so before, on Dr. Brown's orders, I drank a glass of amber liquid guaranteed to finish off whatever ailed me. It looked and tasted like tobacco juice. I would sit on the potty until the verdict was rendered. Time passes, and this serene tableau, like those I observed through the side slats of the porch, will join the select views that grow brighter rather than dimmer. The train that rumbles past does so in silence. A cloud of dust sparkles over the empty crossing. I hear the subdued voice of Anna as she speaks to Dr. Brown, as if muttering a prayer. Unaccountably, he chuckles. He has never had a tapeworm, or sat for hours on a potty at an open window.

That winter we had a blizzard that left the snow drifted as high as the second-floor windows, darkening the house. I could open a window, push through my sled, and

*The Inhabitants, 1946.

16

glide through the bushlike trees of the neighbor's orchard. A small mound of dirty snow, hard as a salt cake, was still in the yard in June.

One night I woke to see the flare of lights in the yard and hear the cough of a gasoline motor. An automobile was in the yard, the motor still running, because my father didn't know how to turn it off. He had bought it in Columbus, on his way back from Omaha, and driven it to Central City in second gear rather than shift. With him he had a young woman, dark hair framing her face, her teeth white between her smiling red lips. I could smell her perfume. My father said, "Son, come and kiss your new mother!" and I am led forward to face her. She says, "You're not going to kiss me?" Why am I so reluctant? Her hands beckon me toward her, but I am bewildered. I stand my ground between the old and the new mother. Her name was Gertrude, and with her arrival my childhood world expands.

*M*y new mother was nearer to my age than my father's, and we got along fine. She had kid brothers like me, with whom she wrestled, but my old mother, Anna, did not like her so much. In her opinion Gertrude was old enough to take care of herself. It was agreeable to me to have two mothers, but Anna preferred to live in Aurora, with her own people, where I could come and visit her when I wanted. If my father was too busy to drive me down in his new car, I would go on the Burlington local with the butterflies in the coaches. The conductor knew me, and would see that I got off in the right town.

In 1918 my father was in his mid-thirties, a jovial good-natured man with wavy brown hair, his head on the pedestal of a high stiff collar. He liked to josh people. He was friendly, but too busy for friends. His sleeves were usually rolled. I see him crossing the tracks on a trot. I see his head wag, his teeth-clenched smile, as he turns, hearing his name called. His name is Will. I like to hear people call him Will. Level on his head he wore a rolled-brim Stetson that he might forget to take off at mealtime. Anna would say, "Will, your hat," and he would take it off. Gertrude didn't seem to mind. The men she knew not only wore hats, they smoked cigars.

It was my father's idea, once he had a new wife, to supply the Union Pacific dining car service with day-old Leghorn eggs. To do that he would first have to raise the chickens from eggs hatched in incubators. To do that he would need a farm with nothing on it but thousands of chickens. The man in charge of the Union Pacific commissary in Omaha felt that my father was the man. T. P. Luckett liked me, and I liked him. He was not the first man to rest his hand on my head, mussing up my hair, but he is the first that I remember. I liked that. It was something my father had never done.

T. P. Luckett's office was in Omaha, but he could ride the railroad free any time he wanted as far as Cheyenne, Wyoming, or Ogden, Utah. The eastbound flier stopped in Central City just to let him off. He told my father, and my father told Gertrude, there was a great future with the dining car service in fresh day-old Leghorn eggs.

Without Anna to feed and care for me, we had most of our meals in local cafés. On weekends my father would drive us to Grand Island, where we would eat in a Japanese restaurant that served black bread. In a glass case at the front of the restaurant, if the proper coin was inserted, a wax hand holding a bow played a violin. I was given the coins to insert. Gerald Cole told me that the

19

music was made by a midget violinist concealed in the box. I kept this information to myself, fearing my father would no longer supply me with coins if he knew that.

In Central City we had our meals in the café on Main Street with tables for ladies. People seated in their buggies parked at the front could peer over the half curtain at the front and watch us eat. Some of the older, bigger boys might stop and make faces. When we came out in the street they would hoot and whistle. This amused me and Gertrude, but angered my father. I had never before heard him use words I had first heard from Gertrude. She had learned them from her older brothers and her father, who was "a dirty-minded old bastard." That didn't mean she didn't like him. It wasn't at all clear to me what it was she meant. On the side of a freight car near the station I saw the name MORRIS printed under a drawing that I knew to be dirty but did not know why. The shame I felt kept me from talking about it.

Was it perhaps the local gossip that led my father to move us first to Kearney and then to Schuyler? My new mother and his pretty wife, accustomed to life in a big city, sat all day in a rented house with the green shades drawn against the heat and light. She had no lady friends. There were no radios. All she had was me to talk to, and to fight with over the flavors in the box of Whitman chocolates. I wound the Victrola for her and played her favorite record, "When You Wore a Tulip, a Bright Yellow Tulip, and I Wore a Red, Red Rose." I had some boys to play with, in the willows along the river, until we all went to eat and then to a movie. Gertrude liked mushy movies. I liked William S. Hart, Tom Mix, Hoot Gibson and Harry Carey. We both liked Charlie Chaplin.

20

Watching Charlie Chaplin, I got the hiccups so bad I often had to leave my seat and go for a drink in the lobby.

On the Fourth of July we were living in Schuyler, where I spent all day in a piano box with three other boys smoking firecracker punk and corn silk rolled up in toilet paper. One or the other made me so sick I just lay there in the box until my father found me.

On a cold, sunless day I walked with my classmates to where a railroad coach had been parked on a siding. Inside the coach it was dark, but the shining steel blades of swords and bayonets reflected the dim light. The coach was full of war gear and weapons taken from the "enemy" on the western front. I had heard about the western front, but I did not know where it was. There were shells and shell casings, helmets with spears on the top, helmets shaped like buckets, leather puttees and belts, a pistol in a holster, a uniform with a bullet hole through the chest pocket. Some of us saw it and giggled. In a war with BB guns, my eye at a knothole in a privy, I was hit just below the eyeball by a BB that just stuck there. When it fell out it left a big freckle. I had been warned not to shoot a gun at anybody. I left the coach before the others and ran back to the station to get away from the smells and the unwelcome impressions. The station lobby was warm, there was a scale near the door, and as I weighed myself without a penny I heard the chirp of the telegraph key through the grill at the ticket window.

In Kearney and Schuyler my father first spoke to us as "you two." "What have you two been up to?" or "What would you two like to do?" We were usually of one opinion. We wanted to eat, then go to a movie. We had similar tastes in ice cream and sundaes, but I liked Black

Jack gum better than Juicy Fruit or Spearmint. We both liked popcorn better than Cracker Jacks. When I came home from school we might play checkers or caroms, or she would dress me up in her clothes and we would have a party. In the mirror, standing on the bed, I saw myself wearing her shoes and hats. If we wrestled and I started to win, she would tickle me or bite.

If we met other people, my father referred to us as "they" or "them." "They don't like that"; or "I've got them to consider." In arguments we took the same side— it was *us* against *him*. I often felt sorry for Anna but in league with Gertrude, whose tastes and opinions I shared. She especially hated Schuyler. She made my father drive us clear to Columbus to eat.

Late in the fall he drove us back to Central City to a farm he had bought a mile north of town. The house had been repainted, had a pump in the kitchen, and mice in the walls we could hear scrambling at night. Behind the house were the new sheds with incubators to hatch the eggs that would soon be Leghorn chickens.

Because we were living out of town and had no place to eat, my father was able to persuade Anna to come from Aurora and take care of us. We lived in the front bedroom upstairs, with a pipe that came up from the stove in the kitchen, and if I turned down the damper it filled the rest of the house with smoke. If we didn't turn it down we almost froze. My father lived downstairs, in a room off the yard, where he could keep an eye on the incubators that had to run all night. The farm had ten acres, planted with beans for the war effort, when my father bought it. On the east, high on an embankment, the Burlington local went north on one day, and came back south on the next. We knew when it was coming back because it always whistled approaching Central City.

More could happen to a chicken, my father found, than could happen to an egg. While they were still pullets, too young to lay eggs, some of them acted strangely and took sick. They huddled off by themselves, their eyes lidded. In a few days most of them were dead. They began to die so fast my father had to hire help to bury them. A big pit was dug in the yard, the dead chickens thrown in, then covered with quicklime. The smell was so bad we kept the windows closed and the shades drawn at the back of the house. Before the last pullets died, my father put them into crates and sent them to his brother Harry in Norfolk, who left them uncalled for on the station platform out of fear of infecting his Plymouth Rocks.

The chickens that didn't die wandered around in the bean field until it snowed, and we could no longer see them. My father's clothes were so filthy and he smelled so bad, Anna brought us our food to our room, where we had an oil-burning heater to warm us. We huddled around it playing caroms, which was the one game Gertrude was good at. On the weekends people who had heard about the chickens would drive out in their buggies to see what was happening. It pleased my father that they couldn't see the Leghorns after it snowed. If they parked their buggies near the house Gertrude would stand at the window, thumbing her nose at them. I'd never seen a woman do that. To see it thrilled and pleased me more than it shamed me.

In the second week the bigger pullets were dead before he picked them up. It was not necessary to cut their throats or wring their necks. *They were stiff, yet they seemed very light when he scooped them up on the shovel, as if dying had taken a load off of them. During the third week three experts arrived, at his expense, from Chicago, and took most of one day to tell him there was nothing to be done. Then they went off, after carefully washing their hands.*

Sometimes he stopped long enough to look out at the road, and the rows of buggies, where the women and the kids sat breathing through their handkerchiefs. That was something they had picked up during the war. When the flu came along, everyone had run around trying to breathe through a handkerchief. In spite of the smell they all liked to sit where they could keep their eyes on the house, and the upstairs room where the boy and girl were in quarantine. He had more or less ordered them to stay inside. Now and then he caught sight of the boy with his head at the window, peering at him, and one evening he thought he heard, blown to him, the music of their phonograph. Something about a lover who went away and did not come back.

Nothing that he did, or paid to have done, seemed to help. The hens he shipped off to Harry died on the rail-road platform. They were left in their crates and shipped back to him for burial. He was advised to keep his sick chickens to himself.

And then it stopped—for no more apparent reason than it had begun. It left him with one hundred and twenty-seven pullets still alive. He sat around waiting for them to die, but somehow they went on living, they even grew fatter, and early every morning the three young roosters

24

*crowed. It was something like the first, and the last, sound that he had ever heard. When he heard them crow he would come to the window, facing the cold morning sky, and look at the trees he had planted at the edge of the yard. They were wired to the ground, which kept them, it was said, from blowing away.**

In April we opened the windows and let the fresh air into the house. The stink of the quicklime was gone. In the corners of the bean field, packed around the fence posts, you could still see the bodies of some chickens, white as snow.

Coming back from town, where we had gone to eat, and had put Anna on the train for Aurora, the way the sun blazed on the upstairs windows the house looked on fire.

"It looks on fire!" I said.

Gertrude said, "I wish to Christ it was!"

We were still in the car, parked beside the house, when my father asked us, "Where would you two like to live?"

We both said Omaha. We had often talked it over, and that was it.

On our way to Omaha a few days later, the fields on both sides of the road were green as grass. "Look at the grass!" Gertrude cried.

"It's not grass," my father said, "it's winter wheat."

I didn't know what it was, but when Gertrude laughed to learn it was winter wheat, I laughed along with her. It was us against him.

*The Works of Love, 1952.

25

*U*ntil my father found a house for us, we lived in a
hotel near 18th and Farnam. From the fourth-floor
window, my legs held by Gertrude, I peered to see the
buglike people in the street. During the day, while my
father was at his business, Gertrude and I sat in the lobby. Between the plants growing in wooden tubs at the
front there were oak rockers facing the window. All day
long streetcars passed and automobiles I didn't know the
names of. My father's car, a Willys Knight touring,
might be parked at the curb. I was free to walk to the
corner in either direction, or sit in the car and watch the
people passing. In April all the kids my age were in
school, and I saw only grownups.

Most people thought Gertrude was my sister. The man
who worked at the desk would ask me, "And how is your

sister?" and I would say fine. Behind the desk were rows of pigeonholes for keys and mail, and to the left of the desk was the cigar case. A pad of green cloth sat on top of the case, along with a leather cup for rolling dice. If you rolled the dice and won, the glass top of the case could slide back so you could help yourself to one of the cigars. If you didn't roll the dice the girl behind the counter would reach for the cigar herself and hand it to you.

What I liked was the sound of the dice in the leather cup. It puzzled me why Gertrude had given up playing and rolling the dice to marry my father, who did not even smoke. If I was on the fourth floor and leaned over the stair rail, or listened at the gate to the elevator, I could hear the dice rattle in the cup and the sound they made spilling out on the pad. I liked the tile floor of the lobby, the swinging doors, and the men's room I could go to all by myself, now that I had pants that buttoned at the front. When my father found a house we were both disappointed: we didn't want to leave.

The house was near a big park at the end of the streetcar line, the night sky lighting up when the conductor reversed the trolley. I had a bedroom to myself, and with the window open I could hear the slam-bang as he walked through the car turning back the seats. I walked through the park to get to the school, but I played hookey most of the time to hunt for lost golf balls. Five days a week the park was empty, and I wondered why they cut the grass the way they did in parts of it, but on weekends there were clumps of men wearing knickers, carrying their bags of clubs. I watched them tee off. I watched them look for the balls in the uncut grass. The balls were easy to find if I took off my shoes and walked around in the tall grass barefoot. If the balls were not dented I sold them back to the players. With this money I bought pop, candy and marbles, which I told Gertrude I had won playing "keeps." Gertrude's family lived in Omaha, but they were not people she liked to visit. Her older sister, Evelyn, worked at the cigar counter at the Paxton Hotel, on 14th Street, and went to movie matinees with me and Gertrude on Saturday afternoons. After the movie we might go to a drugstore for a cherry Coke.

My father's place of business, on 11th Street, was a low dilapidated frame building with an office at the front. In the large room at the back he fed and fattened chickens, killed and plucked them, and candled eggs. Empty egg cases filled with flats and fillers were piled along the walls. The plank floor of the room was smeared with chicken blood, feathers and the laying mash he fed the chickens. My father killed chickens by clamping the birds between his knees, slicing their necks with the blade of a razor, snapping their necks, then tossing them to flap their wings and bleed in the center of the room. Sometimes they got up and walked around, like they were tipsy, and had to be cut again. When they were bled, my father dipped them into a boiler of steaming water, hung them on a hook, plucked off their feathers. My father was so good at it he could pluck two or three chickens a minute if he didn't stop for the pin feathers. It took me three or four minutes a chicken, and the smell of the wet feathers didn't help any. I preferred to candle eggs.

My father's candling room was like a dark, narrow pantry, the only light coming from the two holes in the candler, a Karo syrup pail with a light bulb in it. If eggs were held to the holes and given a twist, you could see the orange yolks twirl and the dark or light spots on them. You could also see the shrinkage at the end of the egg and tell if it was fresh or out of cold storage. The creameries that sent my father their eggs always tried to mix cold storage eggs in with the fresh ones, and that was why they had to be sorted. I got so I could tell a really bad egg by just picking it up.

My father could candle six eggs at a time, three in each hand, and sort them into three grades of size and freshness. He could candle two cases of eggs while I candled one. On Saturday mornings, when I came along to help him, he would pay me ten cents a case for the eggs I candled, and five cents for each plucked chicken.

I hated picking chickens, but I liked to be with my father in the candling room. He worked with his coat off, his Stetson hat on, his sleeves turned back on his forearms, a sliver from one of the egg cases wagging at the corner of his mouth. While he candled eggs he would whistle or hum snatches of tunes. Right after breakfast he might talk to me about his plans to make a deal with all the state's creameries to send him their eggs. He planned to expand, with a store in Fremont, and maybe another one in Columbus. He planned to get his own truck so he wouldn't have to use the back seat of the Willys Knight for deliveries. If he got worked up he would pause in his candling to chip the dung off one of the eggs with his thumbnail. To candle eggs you lean your front against one of the cases and get excelsior and splinters in your vest and pants front. My father bought a pair of coveralls to avoid this, but they were hard to pull on over his pants, and even harder to pull off. They were also hot to wear in muggy summer weather. What we both disliked about candling was having to break the cracked and the not-so-good eggs into a big tin pail we sold to the bakeries. Some of these eggs were so rotten I had to hold my breath while I fished them out of the pail. A really bad egg gives off heat, which you can feel in your fingers, and might explode in your hand if you aren't careful with it. I buried these eggs in a hole I dug at the rear of the shop.

I was so reluctant to work for my father I might pretend to be sick. One reason was I would rather not work at all on Saturdays, when baseball games were played in the park, and the other reason was that his contracts were not binding. Having promised me ten cents a case, he wouldn't happen to have the change in his pocket, and would *owe* it to me. It soon got so he owed me so much neither of us liked to bring it up.

In the candling room, smelling of cracked eggs and excelsior, the scorched smell given off by the candler, my father was a ponderable presence, more than a voice, more than a father. The light flashed on, then off, his face. I heard the eggs drop into the fillers. In the intense beams of light from the candler the air was thick as water. Many things swam in it. Inside the egg the yolk twirled, there was an eye like a hatpin, there was a lumpish cloud soon to be a chicken, there was a visible shrinkage, indicating age, all revealed in the light beam. I was not well paid, but I was well schooled, and would not soon forget what I had learned.

Saturday afternoons, given my freedom, I would go

30

over to Douglas Street and make my way from pawnshop to pawnshop, appraising and comparing the watches. The choice was wide. Silver watches, wound with a key, so large they would not squeeze into my watch pocket. Gold watches with engraved cases, the lid flipping open when the stem was pressed. Watches with seven jewels, with seventeen jewels, with twenty-one jewels and five adjustments. If the lid of the case was unscrewed, one could look at the ticking movement. I had gone that far. I had asked to look at the works. The ultimate in watches, worn by conductors to determine a train's arrival and departure, might have twenty-three jewels, five adjustments and the minutes as well as the hours printed on the dials. A railroad watch. Pending a purchase, I was wearing a dollar Ingersoll.

On the north side of 14th and Douglas began the movies and girlie shows. I liked to look at the buxom ladies in black tights, but I had been cautioned that inside, in the dark, anything might happen. There were men who picked up boys. What then happened? My fear was greater than my curiosity. I tipped the scales at seventy-four pounds, and was known to bleed easily when hit.

The Moon, a movie house that featured Westerns, was both cheaper and not so dangerous. Along with Tom Mix, Bill Hart or Hoot Gibson I might see the latest installment of Pearl White, last seen trapped in the pit with the octopus.

I might watch the serial twice, then have an Eskimo Pie before I went to sit in the lobby of the Paxton and wait for Gertrude and my father. Sometimes my father might be there at the cigar counter talking with Ger-

31

trude's sister Evelyn while he waited for us. Gertrude was a very pretty girl that boys and men whistled at, but Evelyn was a woman. When she leaned over to give me gum or candy, I would smell her perfume and the Sen Sen on her breath. I had seen women like her in the movies Gertrude liked better than I did. She was dark, like Pola Negri, and smoked cubebs when she wasn't working. My father said it was the smoking that made her voice so low and hoarse.

In her apartment on Dodge Street, which I had visited with Gertrude, Evelyn had a piano draped with a shawl, lamps fringed with beaded tassels, and the smell of incense. She liked it dark, and wore a wide-brimmed hat that concealed most of her face but not her lips. If she gave me money I would carry it around in my watch pocket, reluctant to spend it.

One day in the summer I came back from the park to find the kitchen floor strewn with broken dishes and glasses, one of the side windows broken where pots and pans had been thrown into the yard. In their upstairs bedroom the bureau drawers had been emptied, some of her clothes ripped and torn, the bedsheets slashed, face powder and talcum spilled over the rugs, trash and towels stuffed in the bowl of the toilet. I didn't want to be home when my father returned, so I hid under the bleacher seats in the park. I thought the night would never end. When the last trolley went back into town, I crawled into the sandbox and slept with the lid down. In the early dawn light I took a walk through the woods on the west bluffs of the Missouri, from where I could see the sunrise on the muddy water. To have seen the force of a woman's rage filled me with awe and pleasurable apprehension. With my father I was learning about eggs. All by myself I was learning about life.

On top of the papers, perhaps to keep them from blowing, was a heavy glass ball with a castle inside, and when he took this ball and shook it, the castle would disappear. Quite a bit the way a farmhouse on the plains would disappear in a storm. He liked to sit there, holding this ball, until the storm had passed, the sky would clear, and he would see that the fairy castle with the waving red flags was still there. *

My father was not a religious man, but he accepted as a law that a sinner would one day get his comeuppance, and he had got his. It might have been worse. One room upstairs and three rooms downstairs had been left untouched.

We were soon back in the Maxwell Hotel on Farnam Street, where I still knew some of the people in the lobby. When they asked me about my sister I said that she had gone to work. My father had learned quite a bit about the egg and chicken business, so we took our meals in cafés that gave us meal tickets for chickens and eggs. We had meal tickets for all parts of Omaha except downtown. In one my father called the "greasy spoon" we always ate baked heart and dressing, a specialty. I liked to eat with my father and listen to him talk to the cook behind the counter or the man seated beside him. It flattered most strangers to receive his attention. He did not

* *The Works of Love.*

33

look like a man who picked his own chickens and candled eggs. The coats of his Hart, Schaffner & Marx suits had received less wear than the pants. His head high on the pedestal of his stiff collar, he looked a lot taller than he proved to be when he stood up. I don't know for how long my father had been a talker, only about when it was I became a listener. That was when it was just the two of us, and I could listen to him talking to someone else more than to me. He was not a reader, so I don't know where it was he got his ear for words. It was the words he used that got him the listeners, along with the easy way he joshed them. "I see here . . ." he would say, with nothing in his hands to look at, as if he was reading what he said out of the paper. That usually caught their attention the way it did mine. He had a good vocabulary, but in the butter and egg business he didn't use it much.

In the middle of life, with his best years before him, he seemed to have a firm grip on all serious matters. . . . In the morning there was usually ice in the pail where the dung-spotted eggs were floating, and he could see his breath, as if he were smoking, in the candling room. If he seemed to spend a good deal of time every day looking at one egg and scratching another, perhaps it was the price one had to pay for being a man of caliber. One whose life was still before him, but so much of it already behind him that it seemed that several lives—if that was the word for them—had already been lived. Had already gone into the limbo, as some men said.

There were evenings that he sat at the desk in his office, the Dun & Bradstreet open before him, and there were other evenings that he spent in the candling room. He would take a seat on one of his egg cases, using a thick excelsior pad as a cushion, and the light from the candler would fall on the book he held in his hands. Dun & Bradstreet? No, this book was called a A Journey to the Moon, *written by a foreigner who seemed to have been there. His son had read this book, then given it to his father to return to the library. One day he had wondered what it was that the boy liked to read. So he had opened the book and read four or five pages . . . after reading a few more pages he had seated himself on an egg case, adjusted the light. The candling room had turned cold before he closed the book, and when he stepped into the office it was dark outside.**

My father always introduced me to strangers as his "only son." I understood this to be a compliment, but I did not know why until I learned from a teacher that I was half an orphan. That was only half as good as a whole orphan, but I knew this to be a point in my favor. I made a favorable impression on the grownups in the lobby, having been raised to respect my elders. "Yes sir," I would say, or "Yes ma'am," with a bow of my head. I was a small plump-faced boy with a sunny nature (I think) and a chipped front tooth. My ears, like the handles to a pan, led me to favor caps with ear-muffs, or high crowns that I could lap at a rakish angle over one ear. In this brief period of my father's bachelorhood we were almost companionable. In a suit designed for boys a year or two older, one that required extensive alterations,

* *The Works of Love.*

35

I was shown off at breakfast in the Harney Cafeteria and to the ladies at the Christian Science Church on Sundays. We were Methodists in Central City, but my father felt the Christian Science ladies offered better pickings as wives and mothers. It gratified me to be described as "quite a little man," considering that I was half an orphan.

In his talk with these ladies I learned from my father that he was anxious to get me off the streets and back into school. I was not anxious, since I had all day to look at the trains and games in Brandeis' toy department or ride the escalator in Burgess & Nash. A man or woman might ask me to deliver a note, for a quarter. If the place was all right, and the hall wasn't dark, I would slide the note under the door and run. If I got cold feet, I would just keep the money. In McCrory's dime store on 16th Street I swiped a roll of tire tape I had no use for, not having a bike.

One day I saw my father driving west on Harney with a woman at his side, but he didn't see me. She was not so young as Gertrude, but dark, with a hat on. I had just assumed my father was down at his business, candling eggs and picking chickens. He had hired a man to help him who slept on a cot in the back, kept a low fire going, and made deliveries. He was not much of a chicken picker or candler, since he had lost one arm in the Spanish-American War. He could prove that by just rolling back his sleeve on the blue stump.

The day before Hallowe'en we moved from the hotel to an apartment near 32nd and Dewey, about two blocks west of Farnam School. My father walked me to the school, where I met the principal and Mrs. Partridge, the fourth-grade teacher, who was saddened to hear that I was a boy without a mother. From my appearance and behavior she thought he had raised me very well. I was put in one of the smaller seats at the front, on the right side of the room near the door and the gramophone. Right beside me was a girl named Elizabeth, and right behind me a boy named Joseph Mulligan, the first boy I had met who wore a bar pin on the wings of his collar to support his tie.

Until I entered Farnam School I had never seen a colored boy close up. I had seen colored janitors in public buildings and colored women and children on the streetcars, but in Mrs. Partridge's class James Smith often stood right beside me in the spelldowns. His big feet were bare, the bottoms pink as watermelon when it rained. He had holes in his pants and lacked buttons on his shirts. His skin was black as the underside of a stove lid. I looked as strange to him as he did to me, and in the cloakroom we often laughed at each other. He was so fun-loving and friendly I may have felt that wearing rags sort of pleased him.

Edward Dorsey sat at the back of the class in a desk high enough to get his long legs under. He was a lean, copper-colored young man with orange hair on his peanut-shaped head. He liked to chase white boys. When he caught one he swore a stream of crackling curses, then let him go. Mike Smith, no relation to James, was a boy so sooty black I feared to touch him, feeling it might rub off. He never said a word unless called on. His implacable hatred was so intense it included everybody, including

James Smith. I feared to pass him on the stairs or be alone with him in the cloakroom, but his contempt was so great I don't believe he ever saw me. He sat and walked alone. In the class photograph only his eyes and white shirt are visible. If there were any black girls in the class I have no memory of them.

In the morning we pledged allegiance to the flag, and exercised to the music of "The Clockstore," played on the gramophone. During the exercises, Joey Mulligan, the boy seated behind me, often became confused. He would bend at the knees when he should have stood erect, or hop up and down when he should have raised his arms. When Mrs. Partridge asked him what in the world was the trouble, he said that when I exercised, one of my ears wiggled. Watching my ear wiggle was such a distraction he became confused.

I was at first humiliated by this declaration, but I grew to take pride in it. No other boy in this class, black or white, proved to have this power. Nor had I known about it myself until the excitement and exhilaration of exercising. On Mrs. Partridge's suggestion I exchanged seats with Joey, whose ears were not affected by what he was doing. The fuzz was like a white nap on his pink cheeks and through his brushcut hairdo I could see his pink scalp. Everything about Joey Mulligan was crisp and scrubbed. His white shirts were starched, the wings of his collars pointed, the lines in his black stockings were straight up and down, the box toes of his hook-and-eye shoes were polished. My shoes were new enough, but they were scuffed, and the knees of my pants were soiled and puffed where I gripped them to hoist them on my thin legs. No one had seemed to notice that the dirt on my shirt collars came from my neck. Joey Mulligan was also bright as a whip on fractions, long division and the capitals of the states. When he waved his hand to attract attention he half rose out of his seat. To avoid scuffing up his shoes he did not play in the cinder-covered yard at recess. Nor did he stop and play marbles until he got home and changed his clothes.

*It is spring in Omaha, Nebraska, and we stand in the cinder-covered school yard, facing the members of Mrs. Partridge's fifth-grade class. The class is gathered at the side of the building, at the edge of the red brick walk, between two small trees that are wired to the ground. The pupils are visibly arranged according to size and sex, but certain invisible forces have also been at work. The boys pair, the girls group, and the Negro boys stand in a choir—except for the happenstance that their faces cannot be seen. Their white shirts are as if in suspension against the dark wall. The eyes of Mike Smith are wide open and like bolt holes in a stove, but those of Edward Dorsey were lidded just as the shutter snapped. So were the eyes of Mrs. Partridge, who had turned to speak to Stella Fry, as she often closed her eyes when she had to raise her voice.**

* *The Man Who Was There,* 1945.

39

One drizzly day in the spring Joey asked me to come
home with him and meet his mother. The mention
of his mother flattered and impressed me. I had never
been asked to meet a boy's mother. That spring in 1921
we were eye to eye, but with my short neck I felt Joey
looked taller. Under my plump chin the wings of my collar curled to touch my cheeks. The fold of my pants at
the knee concealed a hole in my stocking. He treated me
to a Tootsie Roll at the bakery, then we walked north on
27th Street to the foot of the hill on Capitol Avenue.
Smack in the middle of the hill was a building the color
of milk chocolate left in the sun. Joey's mother was waiting for us in the swing on the porch.

Capitol Hill was so steep that when the asphalt got hot
it sagged in ripples we could see in the streetlight. The

Cadillac dealers on Farnam Street used the hill to test their cars on, winter and summer. Over the winter, people with bobsleds coasted so far to the west they got tired walking back. The Mulligan house was flat, with an upstairs and a downstairs, and room beneath the porch at the front to store scooters, sleds and stuff like that. Mrs. Mulligan was waiting for us in the swing. She sat in it sideways, gripping the chain, with one foot dangling so she could push off.

"So you're Joey's best friend," she said, and hugged me. When she stood up we were all about the same height, but not so thick. Joey had told her that I was half an orphan, and how he was willing to share his mother with me. Did that please me? I said that it did. If I wondered why the shades were drawn at the front windows, it was because Mr. Mulligan, a newspaper pressman, had to work most of the night and do his sleeping in the daytime. She led us down a dark hallway, where gas hissed, to a large kitchen with a half curtain at the window. She could stand there and look out, but neighbors could not look in. While she was making us cocoa I could hear water drip in the pan under the icebox.

Just two years before, Mrs. Mulligan told me, they had come from Salt Lake City to Omaha. In Salt Lake Joey's little brother Louie had died of smallpox in the pesthouse. I was shown a picture of Joey and Louie wearing boxing gloves, ready to fight each other. Mr. Mulligan had once boxed professionally in Minneapolis, Minnesota, where Mrs. Mulligan had first met him. "The one in the light tan shoes for me," she said, and that was him. What was it my father did? I said that he

41

had once worked for the Union Pacific Railroad but that he was now in the produce business for himself. I needn't say any more, Mrs. Mulligan said, since she had heard from Joey that my mother was dead and that I was half an orphan. Saying this brought tears to her eyes. She drew me to her and hugged me. I had never before experienced the gain from such a terrible loss. Mrs. Mulligan said that if I so desired, Joey would be like a real brother to me, and she would be like a mother. I so desired it, but the lump in my throat blocked my speech. Joey began to cry, putting his arms around me, and Mrs. Mulligan drew us both to her. My eyes burned with tears, and I buried my face in her lap. I couldn't remember ever crying so hard, and feeling so good about it. When we had stopped sniffling Mrs. Mulligan cut me a slice of devil's food cake to take to my father, and Joey walked me back to Farnam Street without either of us speaking. I had a new brother whose box-toed shoes squeaked as he walked.

Knowing that I was half an orphan, Mrs. Mulligan wrote my father a letter that I personally delivered. If I would like to come and live with them, she wrote, she would be a real mother to me. The sum of five dollars a week, in her opinion, would care for the food I ate and such things as my laundry. No boy should grow up without a brother, and if I came to live with Joey we both would have one.

My father agreed I could live with Joey if some of our furniture went along with me. We had this parlor suite he no longer had use for, along with an Axminster rug and two hand-painted oil paintings. The parlor suite had a sofa that turned into a double daybed at night. The outside half, where I would sleep, curved one way, and the inside half, where Joey would sleep, curved the other. There was also an oak rocker with a seat so high Mrs. Mulligan's legs were too short to rock it. The Axminster rug was put into the bedroom, where it made the noise less when we crossed it in the morning. Gertrude's walnut Victrola was put in the front room corner where the afternoon sun wouldn't shine on it. Some of Gertrude's friends had almost ruined the Harry Lauder records by not troubling to change the needle. In the dim glow of the gas jet, which hissed softly all night, I could see the oil painting with the snow-capped mountains and the Indians who lived beside the lake in their wigwams. I sometimes felt I was in hiding, spying on them, the sunset sky behind the mountains as red and sticky-looking as Dentyne gum.

Around the house Mrs. Mulligan wore old stockings that kept the kitchen linoleum shiny, only putting on her shoes when she hung out the laundry. In the early morning she might sit in the porch swing until the lamplighter turned off the streetlamps. Even the milkman would think she had just got up and was one of these early risers, like he was. He carried so many bottles they tinkled like glass chimes when he ran between the houses.

If Mr. Mulligan had not been asked by one of his friends to have a beer with him, which he couldn't refuse, he would come down the hill just about daylight, walking in the grass to ease his feet. If he was thirsty he might have an eggnog, or if he was tired a fresh cup of coffee, then he would come to the crack between the folding doors to see how we were sleeping. He didn't like us to sleep with our hands under the covers. He said a boy never knew what his hands might be doing while he was asleep. I usually had my hands out where he could see them, but Joey had a really crazy way of sleeping. He put his head down low, as if he was trying to hide or crawl into a hole, with his bottom up high. There was no way in the world to tell where his hands were. Mr. Mulligan would tiptoe in, not to wake him, then give him such a whack across the butt Joey would almost put his head through the end of the daybed. Lucky for him, that part of it was padded. The last sound I would hear from Mr. Mulligan he was winding his watch. He left it on the dresser, which made the tick so loud I seemed to hear it right in my pillow. If I opened my eyes and then stared hard at the Victor dog in the horn of the Victrola, it seemed to me the ticking sound we were both hearing was his Master's voice.

Until I had a place at Mrs. Mulligan's table I had known very little about food. At the greasy spoon near my father's place of business I usually ate baked heart and dressing. My favorite meal at the Harney Cafeteria on Sunday was macaroni and cheese with a piece of fresh rhubarb pie. In Salt Lake City Mr. Mulligan had run his own ice cream parlor, where he sold his own sherbet and hand-cranked ice cream. You could always tell his ice cream from the way it left wax on the roof of your mouth. On Sundays we had either chocolate or strawberry ice cream, devil's food cake, hot rolls or biscuits, roast pork or roast beef with gravy and creamy mashed potatoes, vegetables I didn't eat, and sometimes a big slice of runny lemon or butterscotch pie. Even back in Minneapolis Mr. Mulligan had always liked plenty to eat. He made his own beer in a crock in the pantry which sometimes exploded when he put it into bottles. Joey showed me the glass that sparkled like gems in the ceiling of the stairs that led down to the basement. Most of Mr. Mulligan's pay went for groceries at Bickel's, or for malt and hops at Weinstein's Delicatessen, but Mrs. Mulligan said that a man who worked nights had little else to do but eat.

I was catching for our team and Joey Mulligan was pitching a lopsided baseball with a lot of tire tape wound around it, when the batter tipped it and I caught it right on the jaw. It didn't hurt so much, but I couldn't talk. My jaw wouldn't move. I dropped my catcher's glove in the grass and just took off and ran. I ran about three blocks, the last block down the alley and across the yard into the Mulligan kitchen. When Mrs. Mulligan saw me, my jaw hanging slack, she gave me a hard whack across the back and it popped into place. I was sore behind the ears for about two weeks but I didn't mention it to my father. He wouldn't let me play any game he considered to be dangerous.

In the fall Mrs. Partridge bought us a new league baseball and brought it to the diamond where we were playing. "Throw it! Throw it!" we yelled when she held it up for us to see it, but she had never thrown a ball, so what she did was just roll it. That was so surprising we just looked at her, and she looked at us. Edward Dorsey grabbed the ball and rolled it toward second, and another player rolled it toward first. We ran around like crazy, rolling the ball until it was scuffed and dirty like an old one. Something else had to have happened, but I don't remember what it was, and I don't want to.

One Saturday Mr. Mulligan did not come home. At ten o'clock Mrs. Mulligan called the Omaha *Bee*, who said that he had left with his friend Mr. Ahearn. Since they sometimes stopped at Mr. Ahearn's, on 25th and Dodge Street, Joey and I went over to look for him. Right there coming down Dodge Street were two cars, with Mr. Mulligan at the wheel of the one being pushed by a Butternut Bakery wagon. They made the turn at 26th Street, then went along so slow and easy we went right along with them. Mr. Mulligan looked great. We had had no idea he knew how to drive a car. Over on Capitol he didn't need to be pushed, and he was all on his own as he took it down the alley, which hadn't been paved. Joey and I went ahead of him, picking up bottles and cans, to where he could let it coast into the Mulligan yard, right up to the rear porch. There he squeezed the rubber horn on the driver's side and Mrs. Mulligan came out to look at it. It was just a Ford, not a Willys Knight or a Pierce Arrow with lights in the fenders, but there were leather straps holding down the hood, with a crank in the leather sling at the front. Why didn't he crank it? It wasn't quite ready yet to be cranked. The great thing about the car, which was seven years old, was that all it had done for six years was just sit, so that the tires, the leather cushions and the engine were just like new. We could see that. All it really needed was tuning up. Like any fine piece of machinery that had sat without running—like a good watch or Joey's bicycle—what it needed before it ran at all was to be taken apart and oiled. That would take a little doing, but Mr. Mulligan would have the help of Mrs. Mulligan's brother, visiting from Minneapolis, a man so big he slept crosswise on his bed and wore size eleven shoes. If they were just sitting there empty on the floor, we could step right into them with our own shoes on.

Mr. Lindstrom was a plumber, not a mechanic, but he knew that what you took apart had to be put back together in the same order. To make sure they didn't make a foolish mistake they put a number on every part they took off, along with the nuts and bolts, if there were any. They hung the parts in the tool shed as they came off, so all they had to do was reverse the order. After ten days, which was three days longer than he had meant to stay in the first place, Mr. Lindstrom had to get back to Minneapolis, but Mr. Mulligan still had his afternoons and weekends until the time came to pave the alley. Putting the car back together was not the same as taking it apart. He never had the piece he seemed to need when he was under the car. Once he thought he had it almost put together till he found some bolts that had to go somewhere. When the time came to fill the yard with sand he still had a dishpan full of loose parts. He could get the car to cough a little when he cranked it, but not kick back. He didn't seem to mind when the sand trucks appeared and dumped the sand all around it almost up to the hubcaps. Mrs. Mulligan thought it looked like a lawn swing, and in some respects she liked it even better. With the side curtains up, Joey and I could sleep in it.

All that sand in the yard meant that Mrs. Mulligan had to hang her washing in the kitchen, with the floor covered with newspapers to catch the drip. Somewhere in the sand pile Joey lost his St. Christopher medal and I lost two chameleons, both for good, that I had bought at the Hagenbeck and Wallace circus. They were there just as plain as day one minute, and then they were gone. On the good side, the sand stopped Leonard Seidel and his little brother from using the back yard as a shortcut, whooshing beneath Mr. Mulligan's window before he got up. On the good side, too, was that the sand was there when Mr. Mulligan threw Joey through the pantry window. Working nights the way he did, and sleeping days, made him subject to fits of temper. Joey would often forget just what time it was when he was fighting with me, which was pretty often, his voice being louder and hoarser than mine was. The time it happened Mr. Mulligan didn't say a word, either before or after. He came out of the bedroom silent as a ghost and got Joey cornered before he could run, gripped him by the collar and the seat of his pants and threw him right through the screen at the pantry window. It didn't hurt him any, but it tore all the buttons off his shirt.

*N*ext door to the Mulligans, up the hill, lived Mr. and Mrs. Goodman and their twelve children, nine of them girls. Mr. Goodman, a short, broad-shouldered man with a huge head, appeared to have only stumps for legs, like a man walking on his knees. He worked in the streetcar barns and rode the streetcars free. Mrs. Goodman spoke no English, but she sat in the swing on the front porch shouting orders to her daughters in Yiddish. The oldest boy, Davy Goodman, had a full round face with big dark eyes, but very spindly legs. When I came to live on the hill he was having a feud with Joey Mulligan. From his uphill position, at the front of his house, he would shout at Joey, using the secret curses of the Yiddish language, which were pretty good. What Joey understood was bad enough, but what he didn't understand enraged him. His face flushed to purple. The veins stood out in his neck. If Davy Goodman would come down on Joey Mulligan's level, Joey would break every bone in his yellow Jewish body. Joey had as loud a voice—or louder—as anybody, but he didn't have Davy Goodman's vocabulary. I took Joey's side, standing close by with my arms crossed on my chest, my legs straddled. My jaw was set, but my ears were open. I had never heard or seen in a boy so small such fluent, venomous, wonderful curses. He also had the scathing looks and the gestures. Atop the four-foot wall, as he was, neither did he look so small as he would have down on our level.

Naturally, I was Joey's loyal friend, but I was also confused by so much talent. It shamed me to admit it, but I admired Davy Goodman. In his fury he would spit, then grind his heel on it, rolling his sleeves up high on his spidery arms. I could have outwrestled him in a jiffy, but if I didn't grab him he would give me a nose bleed, being quick with his fists.

Davy and his smaller sisters went to a grade school five blocks to the east, near Central High School, from where they had been sent home when the visiting nurse found lice in their hair. Mrs. Mulligan had been stunned to hear it, but not surprised. Mrs. Ahearn, who had been in the Goodman house, reported that it lacked rugs and furniture. Strong odors blew out of the kitchen. The two older Goodman girls, Esther and Ruth, fought over the boys who came to see them. On hot summer nights Esther might be seen dousing herself with the sprinkler, naked as a baby. When Kopfer called the police they came in a squad car and parked at the front of the house to watch her. In her loud, hoarse Jewish voice Esther shouted curses at them until they went away.

The windows open, the draft through the house would bring the smell of the iron, of the sprinkled clothes, of the scorched smell of the starch, to where he lay on the daybed in the living room. The creak of the ironing board would sometimes put him to sleep, sometimes keep him awake. Mrs. Mulligan liked to iron in her slip, the bottom pinned up so the draft would blow cool on her legs, her hair piled up high like a turban so it would also blow on her neck. She did not trust ironing to the laundry. His shirts were an especial problem due to the shortness of his neck, which flattened the collars and made the points curl up. Pins to support the tie did not help. Mrs. Mulligan took pride in his appearance and never let him wear a shirt more than three times, and straightened the lines in his stockings before he left the house. The paper lining was also left in his new caps. Boys who wore their caps over one ear were only fit to be with the Western Union, as they flew past him, furiously pumping, their butts wagging high on the saddles, racing off to some forbidden pleasure with waitresses. *

A pair of unalike twins, Burgess and Byron Minter, the only boys in class smaller than I was, played music on Friday afternoons, Byron the violin, Burgess the piano. In order to reach the pedals, only part of Burgess rested on the bench. They were often accompanied by Betty Zabriskie, owl-eyed, moon-faced, red-lipped, with her long

*One Day, 1965.

doughnut curls dangling down to rest on the cello. To brush against Betty Zabriskie in the cloakroom, or exchange a greeting on the stairs, stirred me in a way I had not experienced with other girls. She wore half socks, exposing the plump knees straddling her cello. I was responsive to music, as well as to Betty Zabriskie, and my experience with Gertrude stood me in good stead when I would wind the Victrola, put on the records and change the needles. "The Clockstore," my first favorite music, gave way to "Humoresque" and Liszt's Hungarian Rhapsody no. 2, selections that were featured in the Music Memory Contest. While the music played, Mrs. Partridge stood at the back of the room looking out the window, or over the floor register where the heat puffed out her skirts. I longed to give her something but scorned the apples given to her by girls. She suffered from headaches caused by chalk dust, and during recess would often lie down on the cot in the nurse's room off the annex. Her bone hairpins were often on the pillow, and the smell of her galoshes in the closet.

In the dead of the winter, during and after Christmas vacation, anybody with a sled came from all over to Capitol Hill. The steep grade leveled off at 27th Street, with a long clear coast to 28th. If the track was hard and icy some sledders might go around the corner to Davenport. The early sledders were usually the duffers, who packed down the snow and cleared a trail so we could walk up the hill. The best sleds were Flexible Flyer Junior Racers, which were low to the snow and tapered down at the back. With a second rider to give the sled a good push, then crouch down between the legs of the steerer, by the time you hit the level at the bottom of the hill you were flying. It hurt to breathe. Your cheeks would be numb and your eyes watered. The long walk back gave you time to recover and watch the other sledders whoosh by you. Where the ice was worn thin on the bumps the runners gave off sparks.

In January the bobsleds would come from somewhere and rumble down the hill like runaway trucks, as many as fifteen kids squeezed tight on the seat. Cross traffic would be stopped on 27th Street when the bobs came down the hill. It all ended the winter that something went wrong and the driver couldn't steer. The bob jumped the curb at the bottom and plowed through the basement wall of a house, killing three kids. One of the girls we knew was all broken up. It took us a while to get back to sledding and come in with our cheeks cracked, our lips chapped and sore, our toes itchy with frostbite, but our blood hot with the fever of our excitement. The week I had a bad felon and couldn't go out and slide I thought I would die.

I gave up sledding for ice skating on the frozen pond of Turner Park. Billy Worthington, a freshman in high school, was the first boy I knew who was good at everything. He wore fur gloves that reached to his elbows and nobody could catch him when we played "I Got It." Billy Worthington had it, as well as hockey shoe skates with tube blades. Getting my skates sharpened took all of my spending money, but ice skating was the first sport I excelled in. Billy Worthington said so. "You're pretty good, kid," he said, and I really was.

In the spring and summer daylight we usually numbered five to seven, but at night under the streetlight we would double that number, including most of the girls but not Davy Goodman's sisters. We played games of pursuit, the darkness heightening the excitement, the climax full of shrieks and frenzied screaming. Racing across the back yards crossed with sagging clotheslines, we hung ourselves by the chin and set the wires to strumming. The night was full of cries, and not all of them friendly. In those houses without children what was it like? On Hallowe'en we soaped windows, rang doorbells, threw strings of cans and pails onto porches, reversed garbage pails so the lid sat on the bottom, howled like cats, barked like dogs, put toads and mice into mailboxes. An enraged neighbor, hoarsely panting, having cunningly set a trap for me, chased me for blocks between and around houses, tripping and falling, muttering curses, until he groaned to collapse in the same empty lot where I was hiding in the weeds. I could hear him talking to himself, moaning. Did he live to remember the little fiend he chased but did not catch?

On the Fourth of July, up with the clop of the milk horse and the rattle of the bottles, Joey and I would shoot off our little hoard of firecrackers before breakfast. The long, long day would be spent walking along the curbs looking for firecrackers that had not gone off. At a risk, these still might be lit, or cracked in half and the black powder heaped in a pile and ignited. In this way I burned the fuzz off my cheeks, the lashes from my eyes, and singed my eyebrows. They would grow back. I was advised not to do it again.

In the late afternoon on a Fourth of July hazy with heat and the smoke of burning powder, Mr. Mulligan appeared at the top of the hill with his pressmate, Mr. Ahearn. They carried large paper bags from which Roman candles and skyrockets protruded. They sang as they approached, which brought Mrs. Mulligan from her ironing to stand at the screen. We were called inside; the front and the rear doors were locked. From the upstairs bathroom Joey and I had a bird's-eye view of the proceedings. Neighbors had gathered on the porches of nearby houses. They began with pinwheels, fastened to the porch posts, but not very spectacular in the daylight. The sparklers threw off sparks like a knife sharpener's grindstone, and we could hear most of the people laughing. Small as he was, foolish as he was, with his shirt off and his pants cuffs turned up, there was something about Mr. Mulligan like a big firecracker lying in the gutter that hadn't gone off. He gave the skyrockets to Mr. Ahearn, and selected the Roman candles for himself. They weren't much to see, light as it was, but nobody knew where they might come down. He shot some at the Goodmans, clearing them all off the porch, then he shot them at the second-floor windows of the house right below us. Some of the windows were open, the curtains drawn back to stir up a breeze. We couldn't see too well from our angle what happened, but we could hear the shouting and yelling. Lillian's father, Mr. Kovack, who had the day off from his Railway Express truck, ran into the yard waving his arms, until Mr. Mulligan aimed a candle at him and he took off. When he ran out of Roman candles he helped Mr. Ahearn with the skyrockets. They smoked going up, then they smoked even more when they came down on somebody's roof.

When the big car with the side curtains came down the hill, we could see the two men in the front seat peering out through the windshield. They waited until Mr. Mulligan had run out of rockets, then one of the men opened the door and called to him. There was a big nightworks display out in Fontenelle Park, he said, and the mayor had sent him to ask if he and his friend would be part of it. He did it so nice, his tone so respectful, Mr. Mulligan sat down on the steps to think it over. He was pretty tired, and one of his hands was burned, but we could see that it appealed to him. Mr. Ahearn had no say in the matter and just stood waiting for him to make up his mind. So did everybody else.

It was hard for me and Joey to believe that two grown men would be taken in by the cops with a story like that, but they were. They both put back on their shirts and jackets—Mr. Mulligan wore sweaters with four front pockets—then they leaned on each other to keep from falling down when they crossed the yard. This little plainclothes cop got out of the car and made a big bow when he opened the rear door and pushed them both in. It shamed me so much to see it, it made my ears burn, and he was not even my father. When they left, Joey locked himself in the bathroom and bawled. All the neighbors, of course, laughed till they were sick, with the exception of Mrs. Kovack, who had had her curtains scorched by a Roman candle.

Mrs. Mulligan vowed she would not let him in when the cops brought him back, which they actually didn't, and the first we saw of either of them was when they came down the hill two mornings later with the milk wagon. Finding the door locked, he sat quietly in the porch swing until Mrs. Mulligan felt sorry for him and let him in.

The first thing he did, before he went to bed, was put his seven-jewel watch, with its chain, out on the dresser, where it ticked so loudly we could all hear it. The first sign of him being up and about was the sound of his shoes being polished, the cloth snapping like a whip at the end of the stroke, the smell of the wax strong in the kitchen. Until he had shaved at the kitchen window, where just his lathered face showed above the half curtain, he wore his snug whipcord pants with the straps of his braces dangling, his underwear unbuttoned to expose the crinkly hair on his chest. Nothing could have been more commonplace, but it left on the boy a lasting impression. No ordinary mortal rose so late in the day and walked around as he did, wearing harness, as if unhitched from the work he had accomplished while asleep.*

A glorious day in October, my father took Mr. Mulligan, Joey and me to the Omaha Western League ball park to see Babe Ruth and Bob Meusel, of the Yankees, on a barnstorming tour. My father had bought us box seats along the first-base line, where we were out in the open and could catch foul balls. Early in the game Babe Ruth hit one which Mr. Mulligan stood up and caught in his bare hands. Late in the game, with Bob Meusel pitching, Babe Ruth hit a home run so high it went over the flagpole in center field. Nobody saw it come down. As

**One Day.*

the Babe trotted around the bases, Mr. Mulligan slipped me the foul ball he had caught and said, "Go get him, kid!" At that point Babe Ruth was just rounding second, and in the confusion, with everybody yelling, I cut across the diamond between first base and third and caught him coming toward the plate. Maybe there were already a gang of kids behind me with the same idea. In any case, Babe Ruth wheeled around and headed for the dugout, but not before I had got a grip on the rear pocket of his pants. I suppose other kids got a grip on me, and in the tussle that followed I lost the foul ball, but I still had the pocket to his Yankee pants. A flannel pocket was of no use to Mr. Mulligan, but I used it to kneel on in wet weather, or rest my knuckles on when I played marbles. It brought me luck until I lost it. It disappeared with the cigar box full of my marbles when I hid it so well somewhere I forgot where it was.

I lived with Joey Mulligan, but I had some other friends. Douglas Fudge was my friend, older and bigger than I was, with an airgun that he let me shoot at birds with. Orville Browning, whose father was an Indian, was a wizard with magnetos, electric buzzers, and made his own crystal sets out of oatmeal cartons. The craziest friend I ever had was Shelley, whose last name I forget or maybe I never knew it.

One day I was playing pocket billiards with him on a man-size table in his grandmother's attic. Never before had I played real billiards. My game was really marbles, but on the previous day Shelley had won all of them, including my shooters. We had played in the soft dust under the porch because the yard was covered with an April snow. Snow glare had blazed at the holes between the porch slats. What marbles I didn't lose to Shelley I lost in the dust. He gave me some of them back so we could go on playing, but it wasn't the same, and he felt it.

"You're no good at marbles," he said, "let's play billiards." At the back of the lunchroom across from school hooded lamps hung over the tables, sucking up the smoke. On the wires overhead there were counters that the players pushed around with their cues.

Just above his right knee Shelley had holes in his britches where he reached down to pull up his stocking. He crouched with one knee cocked when he was shooting, holding the pocket to keep the marbles from spilling. The way his pockets bulged at his knees he looked pretty silly if he wasn't playing marbles.

In a serious discussion he would twist his cap around so the bill was at the back, like a racing driver. On his shooting hand his knuckles were always chapped and sore. He was a shark. No matter what he played, he played for keeps.

Aside from how he looked, he never wore a coat, as if he didn't have one. He would look right at me with his teeth chattering and say he wasn't cold. My opinion is he didn't feel it, which might help account for his unusual behavior. Almost anything might strike him as funny, like a person's name. When he learned what my name was he almost broke up. Without knowing whether I could play marbles or not, he was dumbfounded to learn that I could. "*You* play marbles?" he said. I thought he'd laugh himself sick. He just took it for granted that whatever game he played, he played best. His manner of laughing was to turn away and lean on his knees, like he might be sick, or walk around in a circle with his head on one side, his teeth clenched. He stood still so seldom I don't really know if he was smaller than me, or only looked it, but my impression was he was short and underfed.

Shelley slept in a flat on Dodge Street with his father, but he lived with his grandmother. Since she didn't play billiards, he had this big man-size table all to himself. We each had our own chalk, but we had to take turns with the only cue that had a tip. Owing to the fact that the attic was so narrow, we had to do all of our shooting from the two ends, lying out on the table to make the side shots. Balls that fell into the pockets were sometimes never seen again. They rolled around in the alleys under the table, or collected in one pocket until it was stuffed. Shelley's arms were so thin he could work them into the pockets until they were up tight under his armpits. Sometimes he would do that and then scream for help, as if he couldn't get them out.

On our way to the attic we would stop in the kitchen and look for something to play keeps for. In a sugar bowl his grandmother kept Necco wafers she liked to suck on while she was ironing. Gingersnaps, if they had any, were stored in a crock in the pantry. To make them soft and chewy, the way he liked them, Shelley would put one to soak on the roof of his mouth. If it soaked too long he would have to use a finger to pry it loose. It didn't surprise me much when he said, "You're no good at billiards, let's play poker."

Poker was played by men in the backs of saloons and I

felt corrupted just to hear about it. But I had to do something. If I didn't do something it would be too late.

"I'm not a cardplayer," I said. "I'm a runner."

He had gingersnap dough caked around his teeth, and his tongue worked at it as he looked at me. "You're a *what?*" he said. He had never seen me run, but my best running was done in and out of streetlights, where it was hard to see me. Just to take off and run in broad daylight was new to us both.

I did my best running at about twenty yards, but I was pretty good up to fifty if I was being chased. I guess my best short type of run was in Shelley's back yard. He was so close at my side I could see his head twisted, with his teeth clamped hard like they pained him. Right when he was just about even with me he let out a wild hoot and sprawled on his face. His grandmother came out of the house to lift him up and brush him off. She made some ice-cold lemonade for us and we sat on the stoop sucking the ice and eating cookies as if nothing special had happened. We didn't discuss the race at all, or who had won. One thing I do know is, from the looks he gave me, that he saw it all differently than I did, but I could never imagine what he might be like if he ever grew up.

Several months might pass before I saw my father, or received one of his letters enclosing a check for Mrs. Mulligan, a dollar bill for me. The check endorsed, I would offer it in payment on one of the weekly bills at Bickel's grocery.

One day Mr. Bickel returned this check to me because the bank would not cash it. The shame I felt walking home with this check may have exceeded all my previous torments. With little or no cause, I had stored up and nourished considerable pride. That my father was lowered in the Mulligans' opinion also lowered me. Joey and I were so evenly matched we each sought an advantage over the other, which he now had. The first bad check was soon followed by another. My dread of these checks was soon greater than my shame at their absence. With the bad check I would make the long trip to my father's place of business, which I often found locked. If he was there, he would write me a new check, which I feared to bring back with me. What good were they if Bickel's refused to accept them? My pride and shame led me to think that I might support myself. Davy Goodman sold newspapers on 24th and Farnam, and when Floyd Collins was trapped in the cave he made almost five dollars selling extras.

I began to sell papers on 24th and Farnam, and made as much as forty cents a night. I learned that more money was made on delivery routes, and got a route downtown, between Douglas and the post office. I liked the excitement of so many different people and the dark hallways of the boarding houses. I made as much as four or five dollars a week, and gave three and a half to Mrs. Mulligan. It hurt her pride to accept it, and gave me back some of the advantage I had lost. Making real money like that restored my self-esteem. If my father's infrequent letter enclosed a check, I tore it up. To restore my father in Mrs. Mulligan's eyes, as well as to give myself something I badly wanted, I presented myself a watch at Christmas I had bought in a pawnshop, but said my father gave me. It looked small in its wrapping, so I devised the stratagem of wrapping it in a series of boxes, each one larger, till I had a package big enough for a train set. I was so pleased with what I had done I have no idea how it impressed Mrs. Mulligan.

In the seventh grade at the Farnam School my teacher was Miss Healy, a big reddish-haired woman who wore mascara on her eyelashes. She scandalized the PTA meetings, sitting on a corner of her desk with one tapering silk-clad ankle dangling. If she spoke to me my heart pounded. She knew about men and boys. In conferences concerned with my selection to speak to the fourth grade about Honor or the sixth grade about Hookey, or the duties—soon to be mine—of a crossing guard at 29th and Farnam, I experienced emotions that dried my lips. She selected me and not Helen Tylor, who starred in the plays and recited poems, to give the speech of acceptance and thanks to the Daughters of the American Revolution on the gift of a scroll about which I have forgotten. I muffed the speech. My disgrace brought tears to my eyes. It also rewarded me with the weight of her arm around my shoulders, and a womanly glance from her mascaraed eyes. Orville Browning told dirty stories about her I wanted to believe.

How did the fight start? If there is room for speculation, it lies in how to end it. Neither the white boy nor the black boy gives it further thought. They stand, braced off, in the cinder-covered school yard, in the shadow of the darkened red brick building. Eight or ten smaller boys circle the fighters, forming sides. A small white boy observes the fight upside down as he hangs by the knees from a rail in the fence. A black girl pasting cutouts of pumpkins in the windows of the annex seems unconcerned. Fights are not so unusual. Halloween and pumpkins come but once a year.*

One winter day I saw my father's car parked in front of the café where he was eating. I sat in the car until he came out and found me. He looked pretty good. He was chewing on a toothpick, the way he liked to, and started the motor just to show me how the warm air came out of a heater under the dashboard. What was he doing? What he was *doing* was trying to find a new mother for me. He did not want me living forever with a family like the Mulligans. He did not say so, but I knew he was thinking that we were superior sort of people. That pleased and puzzled me since he was not a good provider, as Mrs. Mulligan never tired of saying, and I knew he ran around with loose women even as he talked about a new mother for me.

We drove around for a while, then he parked the car near 32nd and Dewey where we could sit and talk. That was new. He had always been too busy a father, when he saw me, to give me anything but money. I had come up in his eyes, even as he had fallen in mine. He told me that he had found a real new mother for me, but working it out would still take a little time. She had her own nice home, where I would have a room in the basement, and a daughter who was crazy to have a younger brother. We would both go to the same high school, to which my fa-

* "A Fight Between a White Boy and a Black Boy in the Dusk of a Fall Afternoon in Omaha, Nebraska," 1970.

64

ther would drive us on his way to work. Never before had my father given me a five-dollar bill. I kept it in my watch pocket, afraid to spend it, fearing the person I gave it to would ask me where I got it, or say it was counterfeit. These days I was having so many adventures I looked forward to telling somebody about them, but when the time came I didn't, I don't know why.

In the lobby of the Gaiety Theatre on Harney, I saw a poster advertising a hula dancer. She had flowers in her hair and wore a hula skirt, but there was no mistaking Gertrude. Without her clothes she looked plumper than with them on. I was not too surprised to see her dancing, since she had often danced the hula for me. I would applaud and the dog, Shep, would bark.

At the Gaiety she was accompanied by two Hawaiians who played guitars. A day or two later, at the World Herald Building on 15th and Farnam, I came out of the alley with my bundle of papers to see my father standing on the corner. If I spoke to him he would give me some money, but I didn't need money. Seeing him just standing there alone on the corner, I felt a little sorry for him. His pants looked newer than the coat. His heels were so run-down you could see it when he walked away. I could have run to him and given him a paper, since I always carried two or three extras, but I just stood there looking at him as if he was some other boy's father. Did he sometimes think I might be some other father's son?

*W*hat sort of thirteen-year-old boy was I? I got in the movies for six cents and looked about ten. Measured on the door of the Mulligan pantry, I had lost a full inch to Joey in height, but on the scale in the nurse's annex I weighed exactly what a boy like me was supposed to weigh, 78½ pounds.

My father felt that what I needed was two or three weeks of fresh air in the country. His brother Harry had a farm near Norfolk. In turning down the crates of Leghorn chickens he had sent him, my father felt that Harry might feel some obligation to him. He explained that I was now a growing able-bodied boy, and there were many chores I could do around a farm. I knew how to sort eggs, and I could pick chickens. It would surely do me a world of good to get away from the city for a vacation on a real farm.

Near the end of July Harry's wife, Clara, wrote me to say that I could come, if I had to, but with all she had to do I would have to pretty much look after myself. That was all right with me, since I'd been doing that for some time. I would take the train from Omaha to Columbus, then up from Columbus on the local with the gasoline motor to Warnerville, where Uncle Harry would meet me. One of the things I would learn was that Warnerville had been named after one of my cousins by marriage, who had been born and raised in the house that sat in the grove of trees near the tracks.

When I got off the train in the late summer twilight, I had a fiber mailing carton with a change of clothes washed and ironed by Mrs. Mulligan. I was wearing city clothes to travel in, my cap still stiff with the paper lining, on my feet a new pair of green leather shoes with a dark patch of leather on the ankles and toes. The soles were also green and resisted bending, pulling away from my heels with each step I took. They were so new I'd only worn them up and down the aisle of the train.

Uncle Harry was not there to meet me when I arrived. I watched the taillights of the coach go over the horizon, and when the throbbing of the gas motor died, a noise settled around me like it was trapped in my ears. I had never heard anything like it. On both sides of the dirt road that led to the east the weeds were almost as high as my head. Fireflies rose from the dark fields to hover like a cloud of sparklers. The night air was heavy and sweet with the smell of hay. As the fields around me darkened, the bowl of the sky above me seemed to brighten. My stiff-soled shoes flicked the sand of the road to fall into the heels of my shoes. In the overall drone of the sounds around me I was able to distinguish the cadence of the locusts. It began slowly, built to a climax, then tailed off into silence. At the rim of the eastern sky I could see stars. When I stopped in the road to look around me I experienced a pleasurable apprehension. Big bugs and millers flew into my face. I sucked in small insects when I inhaled. Far down the road, in which I stood at the center, two small flickering lights came toward me. The putter of the motor rose and fell as the road tilted upward or declined. As the car approached me a cloud of insects obscured the lights. I had to move from the road to let the car pass me and proceed to a point where the driver was able to turn it around. Coming back toward me, it went ahead a few yards before it stopped. In the dusky light I saw an erect dark figure gripping with both hands the vibrating steering wheel. No feature of his face was visible.

"So you made it," he said to me, then spit into the weeds to the left of the road. What I said to him, if anything, I have forgotten. "Climb in, boy," he added, and I did as I was told.

The summer I met him, my Uncle Harry was a heavy, dour, silent man with his family, but given to deadpan joshing with his neighbors, his puckered lips sealed and stained with tobacco juice. After spitting, if his hands were free, he would pinch his pursed lips between his thumb and forefinger, then give a twist as if tightening a cap on a bottle. His wife, Clara, was a tall, lath-flat woman with a high-pitched voice, who liked to work. Her daughter, Mae, away at school that summer, planned to teach school. Her son, Will, had attended the aggie college in Lincoln and farmed the adjoining acres.

His house could be seen through the stand of catalpa trees along the drive-in from the road. Just the year before, Will had married a black-haired young woman from Missouri. While I was on the farm she would bring over her baby and let it crawl around the floor while she helped Clara with the canning.

Harry and Clara's house was square, without gables, a lightning rod with a blue ball on it at the roof's peak, the windows of the upstairs bedrooms almost flush to the floor. I could lie stretched out on the floor and look out. I had Will's old room, with clothes stored in the dresser, the curtained and screened window facing the drive-in between the two houses. In the pulsing flashes of heat lightning I would see the intricate pattern of the glass curtain, the screen behind it alive with crawling, clicking, fluttering insects. The cats howled and the owls hooted. About dawn I would hear the gagging sound of the pump, and then the splash into the pail as Harry pumped up the water. As he approached the house, carrying two pails, I'd hear the occasional slurp of the water and the rub of the denim between his thighs. Up the stairwell from the kitchen would rise the smell of the kerosene spilled on the cobs. The flames would whoosh and roar in the chimney, then settle back to a steady crackle. The new day had begun, but I would pretend to sleep until Clara's shrill voice cried, "Wright, you coming?" Since I was always coming, I never really knew if she would call me twice.

She wiped the table with the dish rag then leaned there, propped on her spread arms. A few leaves rattled in the yard. Some dirty Leghorns clucked and waited at the *screen. She left the rag on the table and emptied the pan toward the leaky shade. She stood there awhile, her hands pressed into the small of her back. Turning, she looked down the trail bright now with copper leaves at an old man's knees, white in the sun. She watched his brown hands lift Monkey Ward's, tear out a page. She watched him read both sides, very slowly, then tip his head. As he rose his overalls came up with a sigh and one strap hung swinging between his legs. She watched him step into the sun and hook it up. From his hat he took a feather and passed it through the stem of his pipe, then turned to strike the match on the door.**

Clara baked biscuits, fried eggs and cooked oatmeal for breakfast. The eggs were fried hard, in bacon fat, the oatmeal thick and chewy as taffy. After sitting all night, the separated cream had to be spooned out of the pitcher. My Uncle Harry would spread it on a hot biscuit like jam.

My daily chores were to fetch water and baskets of cobs. The cobs could be seen pressing against the windows of the first small house they had built on the farm. When I stooped to scoop them into the basket I might hear mice rustle the tassels. Sometimes I carried a mouse into the house. I would see it later, its whiskers twitching, spying on me over the rim of the basket. Clara set traps for mice in her cupboards, but if I heard them go off I knew she hadn't caught one. She had little respect for a boy as old as I was who couldn't set a trap.

Clara kept about thirty-eight Plymouth Rock chickens,

* *The Inhabitants.*

70

and Harry milked about twenty Jersey cows. The cow pasture was at the far north end of the farm, down a lane of cottonwoods that Harry himself had planted. Nothing I had ever seen grew so close to the sky. Some nights the cows would come into the barn, and other nights I would have to go after them. There was always one cow, when she saw me coming, that would go to the farthest corner of the pasture, where the weeds were high. In the knee-high weeds near the barn I had seen both garter snakes and sand vipers. What to do? What I had learned to do was run. Once I got behind the last cow I would hoot and holler like I was crazy, and once you get an old cow riled up she likes to run with her tail up, like a whip in a stock, her udder swinging. I'd let up running and walk once I reached the tree lane, but some of the cows would still be mooing when they reached the barn. What was it they'd seen? Uncle Harry asked me. He was also puzzled why his cows, with such good pasture, were giving so little milk. In my first week on the farm the one thing I had learned was to keep my own counsel, and my mouth shut. The cows didn't much like me in the stable either, mooing and milling around when I came near them, so I would just stand around the stable door watching Harry squirt milk right from the teat at a row of cats. To make sure they didn't miss any, they would rise up and let it splash on their fronts, then lick it off.

In the yard are the remains of a croquet set—four of the wire wickets, a striped ball, a club, and one bird-spattered end post. On the barn the hayloft window is clear and in the window are several cats—but the roof of the barn and *other details are left out. On the harrow the metal seat is drawn as if copied from a photograph, but the seat itself is in suspension and not joined to the frame. The corn crib is blocked in very roughly and under the lean-to roof is a treadle grindstone. The drip can suspends over the stone as the harrow seat over the harrow, and how the treadle mechanism operates is a little obscure. Beneath the stone, in a nest of dirty feathers, is a chill white egg. The hedge is cut flat at the top and extends the length of the drive-way, with a break for the trail to the privy. There is a heavy undergrowth, and it happens that all we can see of the privy is the tin on the door and the curling leaves of a catalogue. . . . The whole sketch is like a peeling fresco, or even more like a jigsaw puzzle from which the key pieces have been removed. One of the hardest pieces to fit has been the pump. It has twice been put in—and once erased out—for either the barn is much too close or the pump is much too far away. This may have more to do with the weight of a full pail of water—fetched water—than it has with the actual location of the pump. The only solution was to draw both pumps in, reconsider the matter, and then take one pump out. This he did, but the pump that he left was where no sensible pump would be. And the one he took out was the pump in which he couldn't believe.**

When I didn't have my chores to do I liked to sit in the sun, my back against the warm boards of the barn. I wanted to look like a farmboy, my face and arms tan, when I got back to Omaha. Compared to the noise at

The Man Who Was There.

72

night, the day seemed to me as quiet as a church. Here and there I saw a butterfly zigzagging, or grass stems waggle when a grasshopper jumped. Cloud shadows passed over the scarecrow in Clara's garden, the straw sticking out of one of Harry's coat sleeves. It scared the crows, but the shiny blackbirds, with eyes like hatpins, perched on his shoulders. If I listened hard I could hear Uncle Harry "gee" and "haw" his team at the end of each furrow. He plowed with horses although his son, Will, had told him there was no place for a horse on a farm. Harry had sent Will to the aggie college in Lincoln, then refused to believe anything he had learned. He scoffed at everything Will did or said. Will was not so tall, but he took after Clara, with her big adam's apple, her high-pitched voice and unblinking eyes. The way his adam's apple pumped when he swallowed made it look like he had a bend in his neck. With Will's .22 rifle I shot my first jackrabbit, but when I picked him up, his big eyes wide open, I dropped him and ran.

The Sunday before I left, the Morris and Warner families had a big reunion at their grove in Warnerville. People came from as far as Lincoln, where my father's sister May had married a Warner who sorted mail in one of the Union Pacific mail cars. May was my father's favorite sister, and the happiest grown-up person I had ever met. She laughed all the time and liked everybody. All the women at the reunion brought along whatever it was they cooked the best. We had chicken and hams, potato salad and cole slaw, with everything else in a white sauce. Clara had made berry pies the week before and stored them in the storm cave until the reunion, wiping off the mold with a cloth dampened with vinegar. It didn't work for pies with meringue toppings, but it worked for hers. All I did was chase my cousins in and out of the house until we were eaten up by mosquitoes and had to sit inside. Two of my cousins from Lincoln had run around barefoot and cut the skin between their toes on the sharp sickle grass. Not having lived on a farm, or brought in cows from the pasture, they didn't know about sickle grass or very much else.

When it was time for me to leave I was tanned on my arms and had freckles on my nose. In a pillbox I had found in the cobhouse I had the forked tongue of a sandpiper, along with three copper shell casings from the bullets I had shot at the rabbit. At the Warnerville station Harry asked me who my father was married to now. I said I didn't know. He didn't ask me to come again, or wait to see if the train came and stopped for me, but got his Ford turned around, bucking in forward, then drove off in a cloud of dust. There was no wind at all to move it. When it finally settled there was nothing to see.

I was eager to show Joey my tan and tell Mrs. Mulligan all that had happened, but my father met me at the station and drove me back to his apartment on Harney. While I was on the farm one of his brothers, from Zanesville, Ohio, had come to pay him a visit. My Uncle Verne was a plump, red-faced man who had been gassed in the war and lived on a pension. His eyes might roll back so that they showed all whites, but it was something he couldn't help. At no time did he like his bald head uncovered, and he slept on the daybed sitting up, with his hat on. He nodded his head to what my father said, but he didn't talk himself. In the pocket of his vest he kept gold coins of all sizes that he liked to try and balance on their edges when we sat at café counters. If the counter was flat and smooth he could do it. While my father talked to him about the egg and chicken business Verne would try to balance the coins on the counter. He had a tremor in his head that made it hard for him to sip coffee or light his cigar, but his right hand was so steady he could stand the dime-size gold coin on its edge. I couldn't do it myself. It made me nervous just to try.

It was my father's idea that his brother Verne should be his partner in the egg business. He didn't have much experience, but he had a little capital. That way he would keep it in the family. There wasn't much to the business to show anybody, and my father found it hard to drive and talk business at the same time. Once we were out of Omaha, away from the cops and the traffic, he would let me drive while he and Verne sat in the back seat and talked. That suited me fine. West of Omaha there were stretches of road that went up and down like a roller coaster. If I got up to forty-five miles an hour I could feel it in the seat. If I looked in the rearview mirror I could see that Verne liked it, rolling his eyes when we topped a good rise. We drove all over five or six counties visiting the local egg dealers and creameries. While my father talked with the creamery man, Verne and me would have a piece of pie in a café or sit on a bench in the park, if they had one. I liked him better as I got to know him, and he liked me better than eggs and chickens. We had some good times. If he sat in a café with a marble counter he would stand one of his gold coins on its edge. There were people who hadn't even seen a real gold coin. After talking all day with the egg and creamery people my father didn't talk the egg business to Verne on the way home. He might sit in the rear seat, behind the side curtains, while Verne would sit in the front seat with me, his hat flapping in the wind. What he liked more than anything else was the wind in his face. My father cared so little who was driving he might forget to ask me to change places with him, and I would drive in the dark to the Harney Cafeteria, where we could eat all we wanted for thirty-five cents, including dessert. After a long day's drive, both Verne and me got our money's worth.

With his lips chapped and his face windburned, it was all right with my father if Verne and me went riding on our own. We might go to Council Bluffs, just to cross the bridge and look at the muddy Missouri. Verne liked Iowa towns because they had more trees and benches in their parks. When we got home in the evening there would always be grass in the cuffs of his pants. Now that I was driving a car, I thought it was about time I was wearing long pants, just in case one of the cops or somebody stopped me. I wouldn't have much going for me if he looked in and saw I was wearing knee pants.

In late August, just before school, Verne and me were driving north of Douglas Street when he waved me over to the curb. That's what he did when he wanted to buy a newspaper. He got out of the car, then he leaned back in, said, "Here, kid," and put some coins in my hand. I didn't see that they were gold until he turned and went off. I couldn't do much, with the car to think of, and watched him hurry away into the Brandeis store entrance, one hand holding his hat. I drove around and around the block, but he didn't come out. I knew that he didn't like eggs or chickens, and to tell the truth he didn't much like my father or the women my father introduced him to. What he liked most of all was a roller-coaster road with the wind in his face, and then he liked me.

I had all this money but I knew better than to mention it to my father, who would try to persuade me to invest it in the egg and chicken business. I didn't know much, but at least I knew better than that.

With Verne gone, my father turned his attention to Mrs. Van Meer, the new mother he had in mind for me. She had been away for part of the summer, visiting her people in Wisconsin, leaving her daughter, Claudine, in charge of the house. Raising Claudine, who had been something of a tomboy, had been a trial for Mrs. Van Meer, and given her a strong dislike of children, especially boys. My father had explained to her that I was no longer a child. To emphasize that point we went to Browning and King's and bought me a suit with two pairs of long pants.

We didn't want to surprise Mrs. Van Meer at supper, so we put off arriving until almost dark. She was in the chain swing on the porch, behind the basket of ferns. My father didn't seem to notice the sprinkler was running until he had walked right through it. "Jesuschrist!" he said, one of his favorite expressions.

"Is that setting your son a good example?" Mrs. Van Meer said.

My father said, "Come and meet your new mother," and I walked around the sprinkler to the porch, my new crepe-soled shoes squeaking. She stayed in the swing, the streetlight dappling her face. I liked the way her braids of hair went around her head, but her round moonface and wide lipless mouth made me think of Happy Hooligan in the comics. My father said, "He's grown since I last saw him. He'll soon be the biggest one in the family!"

"I wish I thought so," Mrs. Van Meer replied, and looked through the open window to the back of the house. A short fat girl and a tall young man were in the kitchen, washing and drying dishes. I could hear the girl laugh like she was being tickled, and I liked her laugh. My father said the way I was growing up it would be good for me to have an older sister. While my father talked Mrs. Van Meer looked at me. The wire basket of ferns that hung between the posts had just been watered, and dripped on the porch rail. My father took off his coat, folding it across his lap so the lining and the label were on the outside. When he stopped talking we could hear Claudine giggle and laugh.

I would have Claudine's old room in the basement, with the door at the back I would have to keep locked. To get to my room, Mrs. Van Meer explained, I wouldn't come in the front door and walk through the house, but go around the house to the door at the rear. My father would show me where my room was. The grass at the side of the house had also been sprinkled, and we got our shoes wet walking through it. The basement was small, but had a smooth cement floor and was clean as a gym. Claudine's old room was large enough, but the only window was at the back, up too high to look out of. On the wall she had pictures of dogs and movie stars, and a map of a camp she went to in Wisconsin. She had an almost new girl's bicycle with a basket strapped to the handlebars. There was also a sink and a toilet in the basement so I wouldn't have to run up and down the stairs.

I was about ready for bed when Claudine came down to meet me and saw how tanned my feet and arms were. She wet her finger at her lips and rubbed it on my arm to see if the tan rubbed off. Claudine was a fat girl, with a face like a kewpie, and I could tell she liked to fool around.

"Why can't we sleep together," she said, "since we're brother and sister?" She took my hand in her fat one, said, "You like my mother? I don't like her. I don't blame your father for marrying her for her money." She gave me a quick peck on the lips, said, "I've always wanted a brother. Are you going to protect me?" I couldn't tell if she was joking or meant it. She felt my bicep muscle, said, "You're strong, aren't you?" Was it my new long pants? From the top of the stairs her mother called, "Oh, Claudine!"

"She thinks we're down here doing something dirty. You want to?"

My lips dry, I shook my head. No, I didn't want to. I was also at a loss as to how we might do it. On the stairs we could hear her mother's steps, and we just stood there, almost but not quite touching, until she came to the door and saw us. With a big squeal Claudine gave me a push and I fell on the bed.

In the morning, washing dishes, Mrs. Van Meer asked me what I thought of my father's business. Against her better judgment she had been persuaded to invest some of Mr. Van Meer's savings in it. My father made a very good impression on some people, and was plainly smarter than most of them, but Mrs. Van Meer was troubled about his business transactions. He had *been* in business. Why should he need help from her?

Only with Gertrude had I been talked to as a person who might know something worth knowing. Mrs. Van Meer didn't seem to feel that my age handicapped me. He was my father. I had known him all of fifteen years. We were eye to eye, cleaning up after breakfast, and we put all the dishes back into the cupboard, the silver back into the drawer. I was pleased to be asked my opinion, but troubled as to what it should be. In the egg and chicken business my father did not seem to prosper, smart as he was. Just recently he had found it hard to pay my board of five dollars a week. How could I recommend him? Whose side was I on? Mrs. Van Meer was a short, plump woman of the sort my father described as dumpy, but she was now my new mother. She wore a net over her hair and a bathrobe that she held gripped at her throat. While talking to me she moved around the kitchen wiping off the counters with a damp rag. Mr. Van Meer had been dead for seven years. Living with Claudine, she had grown accustomed to talking with people not much older than I was. Claudine had encouraged her to marry my father. "You better do it while you can, Mom," she told her. Mrs. Van Meer had not personally felt any need to do it one way or the other. My father had insisted. She had not known what to do. And for a year now Claudine had been going with this young man who worked at the soda fountain in the Blackstone Hotel. His name was Max Cohn. He was of Jewish extraction. He made a salary of twelve dollars a week. If Claudine married him, as she planned, when she was old enough in November, the next thing she knew she would bring him home to live in the house.

Mrs. Van Meer liked to walk around as she talked. I sat at the table in the kitchen. Her voice would come to me from the bathroom, or from the hallway where she was dusting. Did it occur to me that in marrying my father she had hoped to head off Claudine marrying Max Cohn? I recognized that she faced bewildering decisions. If the advice I gave her was not what she wanted to hear she would just not come back from where she had walked off to. At first I thought she had gone to the bathroom, but that wasn't it.

At a gym class in the high school I stood in a long line waiting to have my throat looked at and my heart tested, when I saw Joey Mulligan in the line ahead of me. He had grown at least an inch taller than I was, but he was still wearing knee pants and high-top hook-and-eye shoes. I wanted to speak to him, but it confused me to have a new mother, a new home and a sister, with a life so different than my old one. I watched him exercise for the heart test, and saw his neck and ears get red just the way they used to. There were things he had of mine that I still wanted, like the cigar box of marbles including agates and puries, and my Flexible Flyer Junior Racer under his porch. I missed the nights under the streetlight, but if Lillian knew I was wearing long pants when we played "Run Sheep Run" it wouldn't be the same.

During Christmas vacation I was in the Brandeis store trying to make up my mind what I wanted for Christmas, when I saw Gertrude, followed by my father, come out of an elevator. Her arms were full of packages. My father was smiling, his head wagging from side to side with what he was thinking, and he held her arm as they walked toward the door, the unbuckled tops of her galoshes flapping. For just as long as I stood there I hardly knew just who, or where, I was.

In January we had a blizzard so bad Max Cohn couldn't get his Ford to start, and I went to school with Claudine on the streetcar. On the way home I would take a transfer and go down to 11th Street to help my father. I might candle some eggs, or address postcards to the egg and chicken dealers all over the state. Sometimes my father wouldn't be there, the front door locked, and I would walk up Harney Street to the Y and play Ping-Pong until time for supper. My father had become so uncertain about his meals, Mrs. Van Meer had suggested he should eat in restaurants. Sometimes I saw him in the café on 24th Street where we both used the same meal ticket. I learned from Claudine that there were nights he didn't come home at all. I got to like Max Cohn during the evenings we worked together on the superheterodyne radio he was building. The tubes alone cost him five dollars apiece. At school I had gone out for the wrestling team because it was something I was pretty good at. I made the team in the ninety-five-pound class. With my skinny legs I looked so little like a wrestler the coach said it proved to be to my advantage. My opponent, sizing me up in tights, got overconfident. I won all my matches up through January, when I didn't feel so good in the regional finals. Three or four minutes after the bout had started the referee stopped it and called over the coach. I was wearing black tights, but on my arms and chest I was speckled with red splotches. My forehead was hot, and back in the locker room a doctor told me I had chicken pox. He gave me a ride home in his car, and I was in bed when Claudine came downstairs and found me. I guess I looked pretty funny, the way she laughed. The five or six days I was in bed I read *Silas Marner, The Count of Monte Cristo* and almost all of *The Three Musketeers,* and wrote a report. I hadn't seen my father for more than a week. When I was able to get around I went to his place of business, which was locked up tight, with a sheriff's notice on the door. Someone had come to take away the chickens, but otherwise everything was pretty much as usual. One of my father's ledgers was open on the desk, with a package of gingersnaps. The coveralls he wore when he was picking chickens were on a hook on the wall.

Thanks to my Uncle Verne, I had plenty of money, but if I tried to spend it, it would make people suspicious. I might have spent the night in the lobby of the YMCA, behind one of the big chairs or couches, but when I thought about where I would feel safe I could only think of Miss Healy's classroom, on the second floor. When I cleaned the erasers on the fire escape I sometimes left the fire escape window unlatched. That way I could come back later and sit at her desk. It was the empty room that pleased me: the rows of shiny-topped desks, the high bare windows, the shadows of the trees moving on the ceiling. I often weighed myself on the scales in the nurse's annex, or sat on the sheet-covered couch.

Never before had I seen the room at night. The lights

of the passing cars skipped from window to window and lit up the rack of maps, the writing on the blackboards. I could see the white dog in the horn of the Victrola. I could have it all to myself, but the window was locked. Just a few months before, I had been anxious to get out of grade school and into high school, but now I longed to be back in my seat at the front, so close to Miss Healy I could smell her perfume when she walked up and down. Across the aisle from me sat Pauline Myers, her eyes like a goldfish when she wore her glasses. In the dark under the stairs of Helen Minor's house I had kissed her when we played spin the milk bottle. Where had Betty Zabriskie gone with her cello? Or LaRue Gator, who drew galloping horses ridden by cowboys and Indians? Or Victor Musselman's sister, Glavina, who read from *Current Events* on Tuesdays. I had given up reading when confronted with the word "catastrophe." Alone in the cloakroom with Miss Healy, she would tell me what she expected of me, the smell of Sen Sen on her breath.

Between the passing cars the room went dark, as if erased from the blackboard. I had shamelessly bawled to please Mrs. Mulligan when she grieved for her son who had died in a pesthouse, but it shamed me to cry real, smarting tears for myself. On my tear-filmed eyes the approaching car lights exploded like stars. I thought I might go to Turner Park and crawl under the porch of the skate house, where whoever found me, even Mrs. Van Meer, might feel sorry for me. I had become more of a whole orphan than a half one, and I huddled with my back to the brick wall that glowed faintly with the chalk dust where I slapped the erasers. I still had the key to Mrs.

Van Meer's basement, warm with the heat from the furnace, and I could pretend, if she asked me, that I didn't know what had happened to my father. I ran most of the way to keep warm. Down the street from her house, under the lamp on the corner, I could see that Max Cohn's Ford was parked at the front. That could only mean that Max and Claudine had moved into my room. I was there on the corner, wondering what to do next, when a touring car with side curtains pulled to the curb and honked at me. I didn't recognize the car, a Big Six Studebaker, but the man at the wheel was my father. When I got in he said, "How you like it, kid?"

We drove back into town to a café on Farnam where we could eat on one of his meal tickets. It was so late we both had breakfast. To the cook my father said that Omaha was proving to be something of a disappointment, and that he was now looking for greener pastures. And where is that? said the cook. My father didn't say, but he later explained that it was none of the cook's business. He knew where they were, and that's where we were going as soon as he could settle a few accounts. We drove around for a while, just waiting for daylight, then he let me drive just to get the feel of it. I drove to Capitol Avenue, where I shifted to second before we came down it, the front blinds drawn at the Mulligan windows and the gas jet glowing in the hallway. I wanted to honk, but I didn't. My father had rented a room on South 16th Street in a building where I had once delivered papers, which I thought was interesting, but I didn't bring it up.

My father thought I was going to school, but what I did most of the time was play hookey. I walked around the streets, the aisles of the stores, or played Ping-Pong at the Y when it was open. I probably played Ping-Pong better than I did anything else. In baseball I could catch, even when the batter swung at the ball, but I could only bounce it to second base. I could wrestle, but I didn't really like to, and I hated to box. I could run like a rabbit for about twenty yards, then the runners behind would catch up and go by me. I was also good at pull-ups, which I did for twelve times in Miss Healy's seventh-grade class, but what I looked forward to was running the mile in college. I had read about that in a book by Ralph Henry Barbour.

I'd meet my father at the Harney Cafeteria for supper, if he was not busy with the Holly Sisters. They were not really sisters, or much alike, but in public they had to be seen together. I could see them, if I wanted to, on the posters in the Shubert lobby, or in the alley behind the Shubert when their matinee performance was over. My father liked one better than the other, but he had to go around with both of them. Which one it was my father liked I never really knew.

In McCrory's dime store, on 16th Street, I swiped a roll of black tape without any use for it, just to swipe it, and with money to pay for it in my pocket. I was out in the street when this big fellow grabbed me by the neck, like I was a rabbit, and walked me back through the store with my feet hardly touching the floor. When he went through my pockets he found I had money and gold coins. Why had I swiped the tape? I didn't know. Where did I get the gold coins? He didn't believe me. He asked me again, then gave me a hard slap with the palm of his hand. My eyes smarted, but what hurt me worse was the shame I felt when I began to bawl. He marched me up the alley to 17th Street, then to the corner of Farnam, where he found a policeman, who walked me across the street to the courthouse and up the stairs to juvenile hall. Several boys and a girl sat in the waiting room, but I was led into the office of an elderly woman. She smiled kindly at me. What was the trouble? The policeman explained what I had done, and that my pockets were full of the money I had stolen. She asked me to show her the money I had, and I did. Where had I got the gold coins? I told her my Uncle Verne had given them to me. Did I live with him? No, I lived with my father. And where was that? I wouldn't tell her. If I told her the police would find him. Where was it I lived? she asked me, but I couldn't tell her about the Van Meers, and I was too ashamed to mention the Mulligans. I could see she was puzzled why a boy like me would refuse to say where I lived. I did tell her I was half an orphan, but hearing what I said so filled me with pity for myself I began to sniffle. She used her handkerchief to wipe my eyes and nose. I liked her. She had the friendly, motherly face of my civics teacher. You must tell me where you live, she said, or I will have to put you in the reformatory until your father or your uncle inquires about you. I couldn't speak. What I wanted to do was put my head in her lap and bawl. I think she thought I would talk more when I stopped snuffling, but feeling sorry for myself was very absorbing. When she called Miss Healy, whose name I would give her, and learned how highly she thought of me, she would be surprised. Before I told her, however, I was taken, with the three other boys, and driven to a big house on the bluffs overlooking the Missouri. A high fence went around it, and there were sheds and barns at the back. My money was taken from me, along with my watch and knife, and I was given a pair of coveralls to wear instead of my clothes. At supper I sat beside a boy who was smaller than me, but older, his head too big for his shoulders. He gulped his food, then sat with his hands in his pockets blowing on a train wheel at the front of his mouth. He followed me around but I couldn't get him to talk.

We all slept, maybe about thirty of us, in a big room with a high ceiling where an overhead light burned all night long. The boy in the bed next to me cried out in his sleep. The moment we got out in the yard after breakfast, one of the boys wanted to fight me. We walked clear to the back, behind the barn, where manure was piled for fertilizer, and after he'd hit me hard a few times I got mad and wrestled him to the ground. Another boy jumped me from behind, and they both rubbed manure on my face and my hair. Then they let me up and ran off together, maybe eight or ten of them, laughing like hyenas. It made me wonder if where they had put me was some sort of farm for kids who were crazy. I didn't let them catch me alone again and acted like I was pals with the one with the train wheel. He liked to play horseshoes, which we could do at one side of the house. What if my father didn't come for me? I wondered. After all, nobody knew where I was. I thought of telling them about the Mulligans, but I was too ashamed to have stolen something. Clear at the back of the farm, where the bluffs

89

dropped off, there was a hole in the fence that one boy had crawled through. But what would I do if I did? I had the blue coveralls we all had to wear, and they had taken all of my money. The nights were cold. Every morning the ground was white with frost.

Then my father came for me in the Big Six Studie I could see at the front parked in the driveway, and I could hear his booming voice in the hall. He took me in his arms when he saw me, and the cold air puffed out of his coat the way it did when I had pneumonia and Dr. Brown came to see me. After I got my own clothes, we went to Brandeis and bought me a new mackinaw and a cap with ear muffs. However long I was there, it was really winter by the time I got out. My father never spoke to me about why I was there, and I never brought it up.

When I asked him where we were going he replied, "Chicago, kid." I don't know why, but the older and bigger I got the more he called me kid. We had two chicken-fried steaks at the greasy spoon where he still had a good meal ticket, then we drove across the river into Iowa. Since it's when you cross state lines you get into trouble with the cops, I let him drive.

If they ever got married, Max and Claudine probably did it in Council Bluffs, since being sixteen years of age was old enough in Iowa. I first really had the feeling of putting things behind me when we were out on the bridge, over the flowing muddy water, and up ahead was Chicago, where my father and I would begin a new life.

*I*n 1925 the city streets were paved, but the country roads were dirt or gravel. The dirt soon turned to mud when it rained, with the ruts as deep as a car's axles. If you got out of the ruts the car would skid into the ditch, like it was ice. To get out of the ditch you had to walk to a farm and hire a farmer to hitch up his horses and pull you out. On the other hand, if the road had just been graveled it would soon chew up the old tires. I didn't know at the time how far it was to Chicago, but it took us about a week. Once we crossed the Mississippi into Illinois we made pretty good time.

If a tire went flat, or you found it flat in the morning, you had to jack up the car and pound the rim and the tire off the wheel. Some rims were rusted on, and had never been off. To get the tire from the rim, in case you got it off, you had to have tire tools, which were parts of old springs, along with a hammer, screw drivers or anything else handy. Even then you might have to bounce it, pound it and jump on it to get the rim to break so you could pry the tire off. Inside the tire, if it wasn't chewed to pieces, was a tube with a slow or fast leak in it. A fast leak was better, because you could hear it, but to see a slow leak you had to have a pan of water so the leak would blow some bubbles. The spot with the leak had to be scraped with a piece of tin like a coconut shredder before you put the patch on it. The smell of the rubber cement you put on the patch made it almost worth the trouble, but not quite. Then you had to put it all back together again and pump it up, which might take half an hour. I didn't weigh enough to be good with a pump. My father weighed enough, but he was not good at it, and it left him winded and cursing. He would have to take his coat off, unbutton his collar, and loosen his belt. Then his fingers would be so swollen and dirty he couldn't rebutton his collar. My own knuckles were so bloody after using the tire irons I could hardly put my hands in my pockets. I don't mean to say it wasn't worth all the trouble, because arriving in Chicago, driving through the lights, and finally coming out on Michigan Boulevard, along the lakefront, a street so wide I was afraid to cross it, was like nothing that had ever happened to me. I was driving. My father was asleep behind the side curtains in the back seat. Only someone who has done it the way I did it, driving from Omaha and coming in after midnight, going north on Michigan toward the Wrigley Tower, the waterworks building and the Drake Hotel, will understand what it was like to reach Lincoln Park and know the lake was there and not be able to see it, just hear the boats honk.

On one of the dead-end streets we slept in the car until the morning light burned on the windshield, and when I raised my head I saw for myself the world was round. The ore boat I was watching on the far horizon dropped right behind it, leaving nothing but smoke.

All morning, as we drove around, I felt my father's elation. We had breakfast in a Raklios restaurant with grapefruit and oranges piled high in the window. We watched a drawbridge go up like a street leading into the sky. This was a city like the one I had seen on the covers of Sears, Roebuck catalogues, with great steamers arriving, trains departing, the streets thronging with cars and people, and I could feel it pulsing around me like a great locomotive taking on water, the pistons faintly hissing, the boiler throbbing with power. The white building with the clock in the tower belonged to William Wrigley, the chewing gum king.

Dear Son—
*Have moved. Have nice little place of our own now, two-plate gas. Warm sun in windows every morning, nice view of park. Plan to get new console radio soon now, let you pick it out. Plan to pick up car so we can drive out in country, get out in air. Turning over in my mind plan to send you to Harvard, send you to Yale. Saw robin in park this morning. Saw him catch worm.**

We took a room in a rooming house near the Dearborn railroad station. We got a room at the front so we could

* *The Works of Love.*

93

look out the window and keep an eye on the car. If the out-of-state people saw our Nebraska license they would stop and start a conversation with me or my father. Very few of them came from as far away as Omaha. I met a house painter from Grand Island, Nebraska, who said he had a boy my age he wanted me to meet. He took me to his room over a store, but it had nothing in it but a bed. He sat on the bed talking to me, and I walked over to look out the open window. "There's my father," I said. "I guess he's looking for me," and took off down the stairs. My father wasn't there, but it was something I could say to get out of a fix I'd got myself into. Once I walked right through the Loop, clear to Michigan Boulevard where I could look across the street at the art museum, but most of the time I sat on the benches or walked around in the Dearborn station. All day long the train callers called out the stations. High on the wall were the big posters showing scenes of the far west: the Garden of the Gods in Colorado, the Grand Canyon in Arizona and Catalina Island off the coast of California. If my father asked me what was on my mind, it was usually Catalina Island but it might be the Royal Gorge.

When my father found a position with the Northwestern Railroad, we moved from the room on State Street to an apartment on Menominee Street, just a block from Lincoln Park. If I leaned out the window I could see the bare trees and the streetcars passing on Clark Street. At night we could hear the rumble of the ice cracking up on the lake. The apartment was so big we had rooms to rent out if we could find someone who wanted to share the kitchen. The delicatessen store on the floor below stayed open until eleven o'clock on weekends, but the trouble with that was that the door slammed hard when people went in and out. The newer buildings on the street, all painted the same color, were garages for the cars of people who lived over on the Gold Coast. From the window I could watch the chauffeurs wash and polish their limousines. Two of these cars were so elegant they had the headlights in the fenders, and the chauffeur had to ride where the rain fell on him. Except for riding out in the open, I thought the life of a chauffeur was pretty soft.

*To get to Menominee Street in Chicago you take a Clark streetcar in the Loop and ride north, twenty minutes or so, to Lincoln Park. If you want to get the feel of the city, or if you like to see where it is you're going, you can stand at the front of the car with the motorman. On certain days you might find Will Brady standing there. Not that he cared where he was going, but he liked the look of the street, the clang of the bell, and the smell of the crushed track sand that came up through the floor. He liked to stand with his hands grasping the rail at the motorman's back. At certain intersections he liked to turn and look— when the door at the front stood open—down the streets to the east where the world seemed to end. It didn't, of course, but perhaps he liked to think it might. On up the street he could see the park, and in the winter, when the trees were bare, he could make out the giant brooding figure of Abraham Lincoln. Soft green, like the color of cheap Christmas jewelry, or the fine copper gutters on the homes of the rich.**

* *The Works of Love.*

95

If I walked straight east through the park I came out on the breakwater along the lake. A cinder bridle path, shaded by trees, went along Michigan Boulevard as far as Oak Street, where the sandy beach began. From Oak Street I could read the time on the Wrigley clock. Some of the people who had cars on Menominee Street also had horses they rode on the bridle path on Sunday mornings.

If I walked down Sedgwick Street, across North Avenue, I would be in the slums of Little Sicily, full of Italian boys as dark as Arabs, but if I walked up Clark Street to the north it was like Omaha around 24th Street. At night, on the lids of my eyes, I could see the flash of light when the trolleys on Clark Street slipped the wires. I had first seen that in Omaha, before Gertrude had left my father, but in Chicago I thought of her whenever I saw a vaudeville show. Every time I saw a hula dancer, which was often, I thought it might be her.

I seemed to like the city better than my father, who no longer enjoyed working for a railroad. To start a new chicken and egg business what he needed and didn't have was collateral. Anyone in Chicago who needed anything at all ran a want ad for it in the *Sunday Tribune,* where my father, before he put his shirt on, looked for people who were looking for him. My father wrote to them on the stationery of the Barclay Hotel, on Clark Street, suggesting that they meet him in the lobby. I first learned he had in mind sending me to Yale when he said so to a man who himself had a son in Princeton. These men had collateral, all right, but they did not seem to see a great future in eggs.

Until I would go back to school in the fall, my father

worried about my idleness. At my age, back in the Platte Valley, he was doing a man's work and filling a man's shoes. Idleness was like an illness, he said, in that it got worse before it got better. That was something my father read in the *Sunday Tribune* once he had put aside the want ad section. He liked to read, and might write down on a card words or sayings that appealed to him. In the want ads, where he ran his own, big Chicago companies advertised for boys. A boy like myself could get a job making twelve to fifteen dollars a week, which was almost double what my father had made at my age. Boys like me, now working at these jobs, would one day be president of the company. They knew the business. They had learned it from the ground up. My father did not question my qualifications, but he was of uncertain mind, as I was, which business I would one day head. Commonwealth Edison appealed to him, more than it did me. Samuel Insull, a little wrinkled old man whose picture I had seen in the paper, was president of Commonwealth Edison and had his office in the Loop, right there in Chicago. When we passed it on a streetcar my father pointed it out. To get the feel of the business I would sometimes eat pie in the Raklios restaurant on the first floor.

The company that had more appeal for me was Montgomery Ward, with whom I had had personal connections. Part of the time I had spent on my Uncle Harry's farm had been inside mail-order catalogues, and the section of watches that appealed to me most had been in the Monkey Ward catalogue. Both the retail store and the wholesale warehouse were on Chicago Avenue, where it crossed the canal, just east of the freight yards where my father worked. Every Sunday they ran an ad that they would pay boys up to eighteen dollars a week. I didn't believe everything I read, or that my father told me, but if I had to choose a company I wouldn't mind being president of, it was Montgomery Ward. My father said to me, and not for the first time, "Kid, it's your own life."

They paid me fifteen dollars a week to do what I'd have done for nothing, if they had asked me, since I loved to roller skate. My job was to fill mail orders for shoes by skating around in the mail-order shoe department. By early afternoon my fingers were so swollen I could hardly make a fist. My feet were light when I took the skates off, but I felt so peculiar I could hardly walk. I had to walk most evenings because the Larrabee streetcars were so crowded I couldn't get on. That first night my fingers and feet tingled so much I couldn't sleep. After three or four days the tingling stopped, and I'd skate up and down the aisles just because I enjoyed it, but by evening I'd be so tired I'd have slept in the stockroom if they had let me. On Sundays even my father noticed how different I looked. My legs were skinnier than ever. I could wear collars without the wings curling. I had the money to eat all I wanted, including chocolate malts, but I couldn't eat enough to keep from losing weight. Before I went to bed, which I did pretty early, practicing my harmonica under the covers, I would drink a pint of chocolate milk and eat half a carton of Lorna Doones. But it didn't help. I learned from the supervisor, who was from Pisgah, Iowa, and not too far from Omaha, that small boys had more of a problem because the skates were so heavy.

The supervisor switched me to the wrapping counter

on the mail-order chute, where everything came down from the catalogue department that was small enough for people to carry and had to be wrapped. In just a few days my fingers were cut and sore from the heavy wrapping twine. From there, where the time went fast, I was switched to a counter in the retail store where it seemed hours and hours until lunch. There were times all I had to do was think. I worked with a girl who would have been pretty except for her teeth. Right at the front, where you couldn't miss it, she had one that was like mother-of-pearl, and one that was black. I liked to joke with girls, as I did with Claudine, but if something struck her as funny she would put her hand to her mouth, concealing her teeth. But I agreed with her that if she let the dentist pull them it would be worse.

If the weather was good I would walk up Larrabee to Sam's Café near Blackhawk Street. Death's Corner, which I learned about later, was right there on the corner of Larrabee and Blackhawk. As I walked up Larrabee I could see the flashing lights of the elevated trains, near North Avenue. Right across the street from Sam's Café was the Larrabee Y. Through the big windows at the front I could see the Italian kids playing Ping-Pong, and hear the click of billiard balls when the lobby door opened. But the way these boys hollered and yelled scared me. They were all black-haired, mostly with dark complexions, and I didn't understand what they yelled at each other. Some looked smaller than me, but they were all tougher. If I entered the door to the men's lobby, where there were chairs to sit on and papers to read, I could hear balls bounce and billiard cues crack when they got into fights. The Y secretary spent most of his time vaulting over the counter to break up a fight, or chase someone out the door. As a member of the Omaha YMCA in good standing, I had privileges at YMCA's elsewhere, but what good were they if I was afraid to use them? What I wanted to do most was play some Ping-Pong, then have a long hot shower.

A cold day in November, just a few yards from the Y, I saw this man stretched out on his face on the sidewalk. I figured he was drunk. In the dark I could just make out the holes, like buttons, across the back of his coat. He was sprawled his length right in front of a window with a row of small holes in the splintered glass, about chest high. Light from a passing streetcar was enough for me to see that the holes across the man's back were not buttons.

In the Y lobby a husky sandy-haired man, with a whistle dangling from his neck, was behind the counter. He knew he hadn't seen me before, and in a friendly way he asked me what it was I wanted. I said there was a man lying on the sidewalk out in front. He asked me where, and I told him. He asked me if I had seen anything else, or if anyone had seen me, and I said I didn't know. Cars had passed. He vaulted over the counter and took me by the arm to lead me to the stairs at the back of the hall, where the warm draft of air smelled of swimming pool chlorine. We went down the stairs to the locker room, through the locked door into the shelves of lockers, then clear to the back where the dirty towels were piled into a cart. He emptied out about half the towels, told me to climb in, then piled the towels on top of me. Like we were playing a game, he said, "Now you just lie quiet here, you hear me?" I lay there for half an hour or more, maybe an hour. I could hear the splashing in the swimming pool, and hear the drumming of the showers. When he finally came for me my clothes were pretty damp, so I had to take them off and spread them on a radiator. He gave me a towel so I could take a shower, and follow it up with a swim if I cared to. I took a long hot shower but I didn't feel like a swim. I stayed down in the locker room until the boys' section closed, the lobby lights went off, and the man came down to get me. His name was Al Cox. I told him my name, and where I lived on Menominee Street. We had a hot chocolate together, on North Avenue, where he explained that the man had been shot by gangsters, and it was just our good luck that nobody had seen me. It was not lost on me that he had said *our*. I was a member of the Y, but I knew that he meant to be saying more than that. He walked me up North Avenue to Sedgwick Street, where we agreed that I would see him tomorrow, then I made it pretty quick to Menominee, where the delicatessen was still open. Although I didn't really like it, I had a cake of Fleischmann's yeast with my pint of milk.

The next day I played Ping-Pong with Al Cox in the lobby and beat him. I also beat the others I played with, including Emmanuel Guagliardo, a boy so hoarse voiced he just grunted. After losing to me three times he stepped on the Ping-Pong ball and broke the handle off the paddle. When Al Cox tried to catch him, he ran out of the door hooting. But later he came back. While I played Ping-Pong with one of the others he sat in the window watching. He was not so bad-looking when he was quiet, except for his harelip. Just before the lobby closed I played him again, and when I beat him he ran off hooting, but he didn't break the paddle or step on the ball. I walked with Al Cox to the elevated station, where he asked me how long I had been in Chicago and where I was from. We shared a nut Hershey while he waited for his train, and he said that most of the boys in the lobby were real Eye-talians, from the old country, who didn't speak English unless they had to, and they were not accustomed to a boy from the west, like me. While I had a good time for myself in the lobby, I could also be doing good for others by the way I talked, the way I played Ping-Pong, and the way I didn't step on the ball or break the handle off the paddles. We shook hands. He said I should call him Al, not Mr. Cox.

I wouldn't be president of the company right away, but with the money I was making I could afford to wait. Not having to wait for my father to give me money on Sunday, I had all day to myself. "Kid," he would say, "where you off to?"

"The Bible Sunday Club," I would reply. He couldn't object to my interest in the Bible, after all that had happened to me. The Bible Club met Sunday mornings at the Y, in one of the rooms on the men's side where they showed movies. The boys' lobby was closed on Sundays, but members of the Bible Club in good standing could play cue-ro-quet or Ping-Pong for half an hour or so after the meeting.

I liked to play Ping-Pong at the Y so much I would

grab some cupcakes in the delicatessen and eat them in the Y lobby in order to save time. On Saturdays I could play all day, with time for a shower and a swim in the evening, but on weekdays I had to hustle to get in a couple hours. There were more and more kids who wanted to play when they saw what the game was really like. Emmanuel Guagliardo stopped breaking paddles when he got it through his head that that kept him from playing. He learned fast, if he could keep his mouth shut, and when he played with me he was a different person. Mr. Ward Shults, the Y secretary, took me back to his office so we could discuss it. Until I came to the Y, Guagliardo had been the terror of the lobby, throwing balls, breaking cues, cursing and starting fights. He had stopped all of that when it got through his head that it kept him from being with me, and playing Ping-Pong. It was as simple as that. Mr. Shults didn't want to make too much of it, but my being in the lobby, and the way I played Ping-Pong, had made it possible for many of the boys, not just Guagliardo, to see the light. Boys did not learn from rules, but from examples, and it was part of my example that Guagliardo could not beat me at Ping-Pong. The other part was that they had no idea what made me tick. They'd never before seen a white-faced boy like me who didn't raid slot machines, curse, use dirty language, or swipe the bar soap in the shower room. In his three years at Larrabee Y—Mr. Shults had come from the Y in Oberlin, Ohio—he had never seen the lobby so peaceful as it was with Guagliardo quiet. Something about me seemed to awe him. If I would come to the Y three evenings a week, plus Saturday afternoon and the Bible Club on Sunday, Mr. Shults would pay me five dollars a week with the promise of quick advancement in Y work. In that regard he wanted to advise me to get on with my schooling. A boy without a high school education would soon find himself handicapped wherever he turned. Al Cox, whom I knew and admired, had delayed his own advancement several years by postponing his college education. He was now in his last year at the Y college on the South Side. A young man like myself, fresh from the west, should avail myself of the best that a city like Chicago provided. In that regard, my work at Montgomery Ward, good as it was, was not enough. The Y was fortunate in having a group of young men, all from Lakeview High School, who came down from the North Side on Thursday evening, played basketball, had a swim, then met for a club meeting with Mr. Shults. They were boys like me, my own age. They were clean-cut American boys like those I would have known in Omaha.

I wanted to meet those boys, but if I went back to school I would lose my new independence. I had put a deposit on a pair of shoe skates I saw in a pawnshop window and planned to give to myself for Christmas. If I stopped making money I would be back looking for it in my father's pockets. I had time to think about it since the new school semester did not begin until January, and once the weather turned really cold the lobby filled with kids who were not Y members. They saw the lights, and came in off the streets to get out of the cold.

One of these boys was Frankie Scire, who had stunted his growth by smoking cigarettes. He was small and thin, with eyes like saucers in his pale face. He spoke in a voice so low and hoarse I'd have to sit with him in the men's cloakroom to hear him. He told me he went to California in the winters and sold newspapers in Long Beach. He rode out in freight cars. I didn't believe him, but that's what he said. Frankie Scire was a year or so older than I was, and weighed about eighty pounds with his clothes on. I weighed him. I never saw him with his clothes off. I liked to sit in the cloakroom and talk with him while he leaned against the radiator. I can't explain it. He was like a hoarse-voiced little girl. He never seemed to lack for money, which he told me he got raiding slot machines in elevated stations. Coins weighted the pockets of his coat. He inhaled his cigarettes so deep smoke kept coming from his lips as he talked. I got so I liked Frankie Scire, and he didn't seem to mind my trying to reform him. He called me Morse. He couldn't believe anybody had a name like Wright. He didn't seem to care for Ping-Pong, billiards or checkers, and once he'd got himself warm he would just take off, I never knew where.

Two weeks before Christmas I was moved from the retail-store wrapping counter to work for Santa Claus in the toy department. My job was to sit under the throne he sat on and blow up the balloons he passed out to the kids sitting on his lap. Who would think blowing up balloons would be such hard work? It was hot under his throne, and blowing all the time made me dizzy. I would still be warm and sweaty inside my clothes when I left the store.

A few days before Christmas, while I was standing in

the lobby, Mr. Shults asked me how I was feeling. I wasn't feeling so good. He took my temperature back in his office, then said he thought I should spend the night at the Y. They had a room I could sleep in in the dormitory. It pleased me to be really living in the Y in a nice warm room near the gymnasium, where I could hear the yelling and the thump of the basketball on the backboard. Al Cox brought me a bowl of soup in the evening, and the next thing I remember was Mr. Shults wishing me a happy New Year. I'd been sick with the flu for more than a week. My father had stopped by to see me but I remembered nothing about it. I stayed in bed two or three days more, coming down on the Sunday after New Year's to help Mr. Shults with the Bible Sunday Club. When he called on me to pray, I stood up and prayed. I had never prayed in public before, but it seemed to come easy to me. I thanked the Lord for saving my life, and for the new friends I had, for the beautiful winter day, and for other blessings. Nobody had known I knew how to pray so well. Where had I learned? All I remembered was kneeling and praying as a child. Anna had been there combing her hair, and I prayed for both her and my father, not forgetting to ask the Lord to take my soul if I died in my sleep. Praying the way I did was a surprise to me as well as Mr. Shults.

Inside the room was a small gas plate on a marble-topped washstand, a cracked china bowl, a table, two chairs, a chest of drawers, an armless rocker, an imitation fireplace, and an iron frame bed. Over the fireplace was a mirror showing the head of the bed and the yellow folding doors.

*The bed was in the shape of a shallow pan with a pouring spout at one side, and beneath this spout, as if poured there, a frazzled hole in the rug.**

My unexpected talent for prayer may have changed my life. I was sixteen years of age that January, and Mr. Shults felt that a young man of my talents should not be wasting them in the employ of Montgomery Ward. He could not match their salary for the time being, but he could assure me more rapid advancement and time to resume my high school education. The high school for me to go to would be Lakeview, where I would be with the young men I would have met if I hadn't taken sick just before Christmas. Three of them came to see me at the Y, Maurie Johnson, Gene Logsdon and Orville Clark. Maurie Johnson's father owned the Johnson Dairy on Ashland Avenue, just south of Lakeview High School. Orville Clark was majoring in engineering and planned to go to Purdue, where his brother was a student. Gene Logsdon was young enough to be in the boys' department, but I had often seen him in the men's side of the lobby reading the magazines and playing billiards with the men. If he had been married it wouldn't have surprised me. He dressed like a man, and brought his gym clothes to the Y in a satchel with the Northwestern University insignia. His father was a doctor, and he came to the Y in one of his father's cars. That didn't give him a big head or anything, even though he was the captain of the Lakeview swim team. They came to see me at the Y

* *The Works of Love.*

107

just to persuade me to go to Lakeview with them. The only stickler was, as Mr. Shults pointed out, that I didn't live anywhere close to the Lakeview area. My area was Waller High School, one of the lousiest in the whole city. It was possible, however, in such a big city, and having friends who lived so close to Lakeview High School, that I could go ahead and enroll in the school, giving Orville Clark's or Maurie Johnson's address. Mrs. Clark knew people at the school, and if they called her up she would say that I lived with Orville. If worse came to worst, which it probably wouldn't, I could live with Maurie Johnson and his brothers until the enrollment business was settled. They had rooms at the top of their house nobody had ever used. Mr. Shults did not want to conceal the fact that this was somewhat unethical behavior, but he felt it justified in terms of my future and the need we all felt to be together. Was I agreeable? Mr. Shults felt I should first discuss it with my father, who had impressed him as a reasonable man with my interests at heart.

It pretty much bowled me over to have so many fine people interested in my future. I said I'd discuss it with my father and let them know, but the truth was I didn't even mention it to him, fearing he might come up with something against it. I'd just tell him I was going back to school, and that would be it.

Orville Clark planned to be an engineer, Gene Logsdon a doctor, like his father, Maurie Johnson would be an accountant keeping the books for his father's dairy. What did I plan to do? I had no idea. Mr. Shults saw a future for me in the YMCA. As soon as I had high school behind me I would enroll in the Y college, and hold a position on the side, like Al Cox. In talks with Mr. Shults he had explained that the YMCA was a branch of Christian service, to which many were called but few were chosen. His feeling was that I was chosen. Boys just naturally looked up to me, even those who didn't like me. Their dislike for me was envy of my Christian character. They brought me money they had swiped to divvy up among them, knowing that I wouldn't take a cut, but I had later heard them howling with laughter because they thought me such a fool. When I prayed I could hear them snickering.

Until I knew better what I planned to be, the thing for me to do was take the cinch courses, like the history of art. These afternoon courses counted for double credit, and the time was passed fooling around and looking at lantern slides. Mrs. Josephare taught this course, a shawl wrapped about her shoulders as she stood at the window, not troubling to turn and look at us while she talked. Her pince-nez glasses (was the pince for pinch?) dangled on a silken cord at her front and left a deep purple bruise on the bridge of her nose. When she asked for a boy to run the magic lantern, I raised my hand. I had learned how to run the one at the Y, showing pictures of the Holy Land on Sundays. Being in charge of the slides, as well as the lantern, I might stay after class to put things away. Mrs. Josephare liked to relax a moment in the empty room. On one side the windows glared with light, but on the others the walls were hung with pictures of Greece and Rome. Plaster busts were on pedestals near the door, with one of Rodin's *Hands* on her desk. She had met Rodin in Paris, where, to her dismay, his interest had proved to be in more than marble, but she thought him an artist of genius. It may have been the first time I heard the name pronounced.

After school I took the North Side elevated train to the Larrabee Y. On the twenty-minute ride I usually read my next assignment in a big thick book, *Literature and Life*. We began with Beowulf and Sir Thomas Malory. I understood little of what I read, but I was captivated by *Sir Gawain and the Green Knight,* and memorized passages while I was working in the cloakroom. I only saw my new friends in the halls at school, or on the Thursday evenings they came to the Y for a club meeting. Every day of the week I played Ping-Pong with Guagliardo. Nothing baffled him more than my going back to school. He had thought me peculiar from the first, but going back to school proved I was crazy. He was not at a loss for words in Italian, and I was not at a loss for what he was saying. Not that he didn't like me. He was also growing faster than I was and had a part-time job on a pie truck. When he had a shower and slicked his hair back, you could see how much he looked like Rudolph Valentino. The problem I had on my hands, busy as I was, was that I couldn't let him beat me at Ping-Pong. I knew that if he beat me my rule would be over. Sooner or later he would beat me, because he was good, and he had me to teach him all the fine points. When we were playing he wanted to win so bad I didn't think it was the Christian thing to beat him. So why did I do it? The day he beat me I would know if I was really cut out for Y work.

My friends at the Y had names like Domiano, Trom-

batore, Cavaretta, Scire, Giusi and LaMonica. The La-
Monica brothers were pretty well off, and came to the Y
wearing ties and rubbers on their shoes. Vito LaMonica
had a birthmark on his face, but his skin was so dark it
hardly mattered. His older brother Johnny was working
hard to be like me, Al Cox and Mr. Shults. He came to
the Bible Sunday Club every Sunday, acted as treasurer
and secretary, and helped put away the folding chairs.
Sometimes he prayed aloud without being asked. Guagliardo hated Johnny LaMonica so much he snarled when
he saw him, curling his lip back.

One Sunday in March I had a bad toothache and
stayed home. In the rotogravure section of the *Sunday
Tribune* I saw this drawing of a wolf with his fangs
showing. I had never seen anything finer. Using paper I
had bought for my art history notebook, I sat down and
made a copy of it, using one of my father's indelible pen-
cils. What I had done impressed both my father and me.
The next day at school I showed it to Mrs. Josephare,
who said, "Well, well, what have we here!" After school
I showed it to Mr. Shults, who said he had no idea I had
such talents. The Y lobby needed posters. Why didn't I
plan to do them? He would supply me with the paper,
the poster colors, the brushes, and give me seventy-five
cents for each finished poster.

On the front page of the *Daily News* I saw this cartoon
drawing of Calvin Coolidge. The likeness was not a copy,
but it was wonderful. How was it done? In such a way I
fell under the spell of art. Little it mattered that I showed
little talent for it. This fever, which did not abate, persuaded me that I was destined to be an artist, with my

drawings on the front pages of newspapers. I made drawings in my classes, in the study periods, on my way to and from school, in the cloakroom at the Y on Saturday nights. I filled my notebooks with sketches of my classmates. A great commitment fueled my purpose. In the basement of the Newberry Library on Clark Street I found back issues of newspapers and magazines. My fingers were black with India ink, the sleeves of my coat embedded with art gum. A pen and ink drawing of mine of Abraham Lincoln appeared in the high school paper on his birthday. The lobby of the Y hung with posters promoting moral virtues. Just in time to plan for the future it seemed obvious that I was an artist—among other things. Mr. Shults saw no conflict between this talent and the Christian work to which I was called. Quite the contrary. Guagliardo's admiration, noticeably weakening, had been restored. The Bible Sunday Club attendance, always diminished in the spring, was steady. At school Mrs. Josephare referred me to Miss Roth, head of the art department, as a student at that point in his career when special guidance would be most fruitful. With Miss Roth's permission and encouragement, I would major in art.

To get from the stove to the sink it was better to drop the leaf on the table and then lean forward over the back of the rocking chair. On the shelf over the sink were four plates, three cups and one saucer, a glass sugar bowl, two metal forks, and one bone-handled spoon. On the mantelpiece was a shaving mug with the word SWEETHEART *in silver, blue, chipped red, and gold. In the mug were three*

112

buttons, a roller-skate key, a needle with a burned point for opening pimples, an Omaha streetcar token, and a medal for buying Buster Brown shoes. At the back of the room were folding doors that would not quite close.

Over the summer I worked all day at the Y, except for the month I spent at the boys' summer camp in Michigan. I had fifteen Larrabee boys, only one of whom, Peter Deutsch, had ever seen a cow or been out in the country. There were no cows where we were. It was all woods that came right down to the edge of the lake, a mist rising off the water when we took our dips in the morning. None of them had ever heard an owl hooting at night, and they were frightened by the darkness. I would have to beam a flashlight on the ceiling and tell them stories until they fell asleep. Two of the boys wet their beds every night. Back on Larrabee Street, however, they all said they had had the time of their lives, and most of them, including me, had ringworm. Ringworm starts like a little pimple, then grows in a circle and takes weeks to cure. I had it in my right eyebrow, which made it harder to see, but it also took longer to cure. The two Scarlatti boys brought the ringworm home to their five brothers and sisters, and some relations living with them, so they still had it around at Christmas. It was silly to tell them not to use the same towel, and stuff like that.

I felt I'd lost so much time over the summer I signed up for a correspondence course in drawing in order to get the free drawing kit they would send me. To save time

* *The Works of Love.*

113

between lessons, I delivered my drawings to the school on South Wabash Avenue. It was not much of a school. Three or four people sat around a big table, and I could tell they were surprised to see me. One of them explained to me that a correspondence course was by correspondence. In less than a month I went through what was supposed to have been a six-month course.

One Sunday in Lincoln Park I had been at the zoo drawing polar bears. On my way home I saw this small crowd of people gathered around the statue of Lincoln. A woman wearing a veil, with several elderly men, was placing a wreath of flowers at the foot of the statue. Some Boy Scouts with flags stood in the court at the front, and to watch what was happening I joined them. After she had placed the wreath she turned to the row of Boy Scouts and gave each of them a kiss, including me. Not until I saw the picture in the rotogravure did I know that I had been kissed by Queen Marie of Rumania. Nothing like that would have ever happened to me in Omaha.

My father didn't expect me to be home on Sundays, since I was either at the Y or off somewhere drawing. One Sunday Maurie Johnson, with his father's new Buick, brought his brothers to the Bible Sunday Club so we could all go to a movie in the Loop later. On the way we stopped by where I lived, so I could change my clothes. I ran up the stairs into the bedroom at the front, to see my father, his back to me, seated on a chair with a girl in his lap. Her name was Hilda. She worked in the German restaurant on Sedgwick Street. Her unblinking eyes, her head bobbing, stared into mine over my father's shoulder. Her head continued to bob, my father hoarsely breathing, as if unable to stop the machine he had started. I ran back down the stairs, got into the car, and we all drove around in Maurie's father's new Buick until it was time for the first matinee. If we liked the vaudeville, which we usually did, we would stay and see it twice.

I knew from experience about men and women, but from the air I breathed I had acquired my own standards. Mr. Mulligan had been the first to instruct me in morals. On a spring day in Omaha, seated in the Mulligan yard, he had spelled out the distinction between pure women, like Mrs. Mulligan, and the loose women on lower Douglas Street, who lured men and Western Union messenger boys into evil. The air around crackled with these revelations. Later Joey and I walked together, hand in hand, up Capitol Avenue and north to Creighton, until the fever of our initiation had cooled. Joey's eyes sparkled. The blond fuzz stood clear on his burning cheeks. Eggnogs were waiting for us on our return, but we gulped them in silence, easy on the nutmeg, brimming over with the awe and wonder we felt for Mrs. Mulligan. Corseted and queenly, a flush at her throat, she sat erect on the daybed, her short legs extended toward us, the gas hissing in the mantle as we waited for the spell to pass.

My father's practice deepened what was prudish in my nature, a vein that ran deep. I was shocked by the use of words I knew well, and embarrassed by the talk among my friends of things I knew better than they did. Under the racket of the elevated trains I had witnessed gang shags on YMCA mats. Whatever else I was, or might be, I was not one of them. This had the effect among the boys at the Y of enhancing my baffling character and

115

reputation. I often watched, after the Bible Club meeting, the crap games held on the steps of the Y, but my role was that of an umpire. They would give me money they feared to be caught with.

In the lobby, however, where I had to keep order, if I grabbed the wrong kid because I didn't know better—a Trombatore or a Domiano—a gang of older boys might be back later and break most of the windows at the front of the building. Or they would march through the lobby to the locker room and empty all of the lockers into the pool. There was nothing to do but clean out the pool, and try not to grab the wrong kid in the lobby.

Well, that was how it was, and if it sometimes seemed strange it was hardly any stranger than anything else, and not so strange as the fact that he only felt at home in hotel lobbies. . . . He liked to sit in a big armchair at the front—in a leather-covered chair, if they happened to have one—and under a leafy potted palm, in case they had that. He liked a good view of the cigar counter, and the desk. He liked the sound of the keys when they dropped on the counter, the sound of the mail dropping into the slots, and the sound of the dice—though he never gambled—in the leather cup. God knows why, but there was something he liked about it. Hearing that sound, he immediately felt at home.*

In the fall I saw more of my new school friends, Bill Miller, Orville Clark, Gene Logsdon, and the Johnson brothers, and in the big Johnson house, behind their

* *The Works of Love.*

dairy on Ashland, there were always three or four bottles of milk and boxes of cornflakes on the kitchen table. One of the few English words Mrs. Johnson knew, and liked to use, was *eat*. "Eat! Eat!" she would say to me, pointing at the table, since in her opinion I was too skinny. Maurie's younger brother, Clarey, had legs like stilts, but he was short in the waist. He had dropped out of school, which he didn't like, and helped his mother in the house and with the cooking. Maurie's older brother, Andy, should have been a girl: when he put on a woman's hat he looked like the movie star Anna Q. Nilsson. Mr. Johnson let Maurie drive his new Buick because the city traffic made him nervous. He had injured his hand in the bottling machinery and often had trouble in trying to work the gearshift. On Sundays if Maurie had use of the car we would all drive to a show where the audience sang along with the organ. There were so many good songs to sing we might take in another show in the evening. Back at Maurie's house, if his parents were in bed, we would call up one of their nearby neighbors and say that the Light and Power people were calling. Would they go to the window and see if the lights were on in the street? When Mr. Steiger, or his wife, came to the window we would be laughing so hard we could hardly stand it. Only Bill Miller could keep from laughing when he put through a call; the rest of us would be stretched out on the floor, a pillow over our heads to keep from snorting. Right when we were getting even better ideas we stopped.

My art teacher, Miss Roth, might have been the model for the Rossetti paintings on several of our lantern slides.

Her crown of golden hair often glowed like a halo. When she leaned over my shoulder, or took my pencil to make a correction, my heart pounded. Her health was frail. Wrapped up in her shawls, warming her hands at the heater, she looked like a beautiful child. She had done illustrations for art magazines, and owned a drawing by James Montgomery Flagg which we were free to study for pen technique. I was torn between my plans to be a great cartoonist and my desire to illustrate the stories in the *Saturday Evening Post*. At no time did it cross my mind to paint such pictures as I saw on the slides or collected to paste in my notebooks. They came with museums, and were created by people different than myself. My art history notebook contained almost a hundred pictures, each mounted on a sheet of colored paper. *The Man with the Golden Helmet* was my favorite painting. My favorite sculpture was Rodin's *The Kiss*, but I had more sense than to admit it. In my imagination I saw his hand move slowly up her side to her breast, but something always happened before it reached its destination. I was seventeen years of age, and fuzz was growing on my upper lip.

If the night was warm his father would walk past the mossgreen statue of Abraham Lincoln, then on across the tennis courts with their sagging nets and blurred chalk lines. There would be men with their shoes off padding around in the grass. There might be women with white arms in the shadows, fussing with their hair. Under sheets of newspaper, with what was left of the food, some child would lie asleep. If there was a moon, or a cool breeze off *the lake, he would walk through the park to the water, where he would stroll along the pilings or under the trees on the bridle path. In the dusk there would be lights on the Wrigley Tower, an airplane beacon would sweep the sky, and at Oak Street beach people would be lying in the warm sand. The drinking fountain would give off a strong chlorine smell. He would wet his face at the fountain, then take his seat among those people who had come to the beach but didn't care to take off their clothes: who had been hot in their rooms, and perhaps lonely in their minds. In the dark they could speak what they had on their minds without troubling about their faces, the sound of their voices, or who their neighbor was. He was their neighbor. He sat with his coat folded in his lap, his shirt-sleeves rolled.**

Although not back on his feet in the manner he had hoped, with collateral to start up his own business, my father was sorting freight waybills at night in order to have more daytime to work for himself. I would often just be getting out of bed at the time he was ready to get into it. He would drape his pants on the seat of a chair and hang his shirt and tie on the bedpost. In Chicago he had stopped wearing the high stiff collars and wore those that came with the shirt, like I did. In a pinch I could wear his shirts if I turned back the sleeves. He ate breakfast in his underwear, his pants unbuttoned, sitting straddle-legged on the edge of his chair as he poured canned milk into his coffee. If the green holes were plugged up he

---

**The Works of Love.*

would open them with one prong of a fork. The smell of
the canned milk in the coffee almost made me sick. I was
also getting critical of the talk about his plans for himself,
and his plans for me. His plans for me always included a
new mother. I didn't want a new mother, and I wasn't so
sure I wanted to live in the country, or go to Yale. When
he read to me the want ads for men who were wanted,
none of them remotely suggested my father. Who did he
think he was? He seemed to think he was whoever
seemed to be wanted. He was a kind man, and I think he
really liked me, but I was repelled by his ways with
women. How did he ever think a man like himself would
find a new mother for *me?* I experienced scorn. Did my
lip curl in the manner of Guagliardo when he saw Johnny LaMonica? I was determined not to work for my father, and I looked forward to not living with him. I
wanted to go my own way. I did not like the way he
joshed and ogled waitresses, or turned in the street to look
at passing women. I did that myself, of course, just as I
was not superior to sitting in the darkened bathroom, the
blind raised, to watch a shapely neighbor, in silhouette,
step from the tub to dry herself with a towel, or put up
her hair. With my elevated moral standards my own behavior was not a problem. No woman had yet seduced
me, although my hopes were rising. I had little or no
suspicion that my true feelings were precisely those that I
would learn to conceal.

Most of that summer I spent in northern Michigan, at
Camp Martin Johnson. Martin Johnson was an old
white-haired man who lived in the woods by himself, like

Thoreau. He had given all of his property to the YMCA so that city boys would know what it was like to live with nature. In my cabin I had boys who were experienced with camping, and near the end of the summer about ten of us made a long canoe trip on the Little Manistee. We had to canoe in some really fast water, and spend the nights in the open, fighting mosquitoes. When we had to portage the canoes, which was often, mosquitoes would settle in a swarm between our shoulder blades, where we couldn't reach them. I had never been in real wild woods before, or lived on nothing but fig newtons and river water. The trip was marred for me by the way my companion liked to talk about girls while he was paddling. He couldn't seem to get girls off his mind, even out there in the woods. What he wanted to do was get a girl he knew all alone in the woods, in his canoe. Suppose it was your own sister? I asked him. Who would ever go camping with his sister? he replied. At the end of the summer, when the medals were awarded, I couldn't bring myself to vote for him, but he won one anyhow.

When I came back from camp, where the air had been clean, and I had drunk the water right out of the river, I found a pair of silk stockings on the hook in the bathroom and I could smell perfume on my pillow. I put my clothes into the camp duffel bag and moved to the Y. I felt great, but it was a dumb thing to do. I had to live on ten dollars a week, including carfare and weekend movies. Mr. Shults called to my attention that the neighborhood newspaper was running a contest for the best cartoon on a political subject. The prize was twenty-five dollars, with publication in the paper. The only stipulation was that

121

the cartoonist had to live in the local area. I submitted about two dozen cartoons that Mr. Shults considered real prizewinners. About a month later they awarded the prize to a cartoon so dumb Mr. Shults complained about it. They told him that I had been the first choice for the prize, but when they tried to get in touch with me at home they couldn't. Nobody answered the phone. They concluded that I lived somewhere else and had entered the contest illegally. What stunned me was to have been both a winner and a loser in such a whimsical manner. In spite of my experience, I had never questioned that this world was good enough as it was, if not the best possible. Could rewards for the effort be so fickle? Up to this point nothing had diminished the abundant optimism of my nature, or led me to question the confidence I brought to my enthusiasms. This did—but I lacked the time to sulk. My sense of loss was too complex to explain, and for the first time I grasped that I needed a companion I did not have. In a moment so unusual I would never forget it—thinking that I was taking a girl to the movies—my father said to me, "Kid, a good girl can be the best friend a boy ever had."

I hadn't known that. It astonished me to learn that at one time in his life my father had.

One Sunday morning, to my amazement, my father appeared in the lobby of the Larrabee Y. His new topcoat hung open to reveal a new dark suit. He had stopped to chat with Mr. Shults at the counter, and Mr. Shults was favorably impressed. My father was a good talker, and he looked pretty good when he was dressed up. Joshingly he explained that he had come to see me, since it seemed that I lacked the time to see him. Mr. Shults apologized for me, but said that my father's loss was the Y's gain, and he was certain I had a future in Christian service. He also welcomed the chance to speak to my father about me, which he did while I played a little Ping-Pong.

My father had a few words with me privately as we sat under a lamp at the back of the lobby. When he wrote me a letter he referred to me as "son," but when he spoke to me he usually said "kid," unless I was being introduced to a woman. Personally, I liked "son," since that was what I was, and the word "kid" applied to almost anybody. On the other hand, when he called me "son" it was usually because he wanted something. "Son," he said to me, "your dad's been thinking we need a new start." I figured that meant a new woman in our lives, which would explain the new outfit he was wearing.

"I've got my work here," I said, to head him off, but he replied, "Don't jump to conclusions." We both knew what those conclusions were.

"What I plan, kid," he said, "is a new start for us in California." That surprised me. All I knew about California I had learned from the posters in the Dearborn railroad station lobby, but it had been enough. He talked some more about how much he disliked the heat of the summers, which was soon followed by the cold of the winters, and why should anybody put up with that when there was a place like California to go to? I hadn't thought much about it, but I began to. I saw myself on the glass-bottomed boat sailing to Mr. Wrigley's Catalina Island, where the Cubs did their spring training. When did he plan to go? I asked him.

That was where he wanted my opinion, and it may have been the first time he ever asked it. In the want ad section, under "Personals," he had seen travel opportunities offered by people who were driving to California. The owner of the car would share expenses with the person, or persons, who went along with him. What sort of people, my father asked me, did I think I would enjoy traveling with?

I hadn't given it much thought, but it pleased me to be consulted. Even my father had learned that I was the one who knew about cars, and could change tires. On South State Street, when we arrived in Chicago, I had seen a battered old touring car with tire casings roped to the front and rear bumpers, cans for gas and oil in a rack on the running board, canvas water bags between the hood and the fenders, the cracked windshield smeared with rusty water from the radiator, and the whole car, including the dashboard, under a film of dust so thick you could write in it, which was what somebody had done. Across the rear end was fingerprinted CALIFORNIA OR BUST. If I was driving that car I would need a pair of goggles and would wear my cap backwards, with the brim at the rear.

Wouldn't it depend on the car? I said. That too was my father's opinion. The larger the car, for example, the more passengers there would be to share expenses. He regretted not knowing about this form of travel when we drove from Omaha to Chicago. How soon, he asked me, would I feel free to start?

Was I able to conceal my excitement? I imagined what it might be like to drive across real deserts, and snow-covered mountains. I would go to school later, in California! I had seen college movies of suntanned boys and girls, in a shimmer of happiness, driving around in sports cars. I was all ready to go immediately, but my father thought I should finish the semester of school I had started. We would also need time to buy a car and make the

125

necessary arrangements. What did I think, he asked me, of this?

Driving Southern California.
Seek congenial passengers
to share expenses. Warm
southern route all the way.

I recognized the cryptic shorthand style as that of a railroad agent and telegraph operator. My father felt that he should run the ad before we bought the car. If a larger number of travelers responded, we'd want a bigger car, and have more money to buy it. He had given the project considerable thought. Each passenger would be limited to one bag, and ladies, if present, should be with their husbands. After our experience with the Studebaker he wanted my advice about the best tires. I wanted Kelly Springfields, but I knew we would get what came with the car.

On Sunday afternoons, in the lobby of the Barclay Hotel on Clark Street, my father would meet with the people who had responded to his ad in the "Personals" column. One of them proved to be a plainclothes policeman checking on men who used want ads to seduce women. He wanted to know where my father came from, where he lived, and where he worked. My father had to bring him back to our apartment so he could meet me. I was working on a cartoon for the high school paper, and he pulled up a chair to watch me. He couldn't figure out a shady character like my father with a boy like me. My father gave our previous address as Central City, where he had been a station agent and run a big chicken business, since

any address in Omaha would show the police were looking for him. They might be looking for me, if they knew
I'd been put in a reformatory for stealing something.

My father was so certain the policeman would be back
we put our traveling clothes into one bag and moved into
a housekeeping room on Shelby. What we would do, my
father said, would be to get us a car and then pick up the
passengers later. Chicago wasn't the only town that was
full of people who would rather live in California. Right
down the road a piece was St. Louis, and just west of St.
Louis there was Kansas City, a town a lot of people
would like to get away from. But my father would like to
see it, just in case he liked it better than Omaha.

In a garage on North Clark Street, mostly used for
storage, my father stumbled on just the car we needed. A
pair of old ladies had owned it, one of whom had just
died, and the garageman was selling it for the storage
costs. The rubber was like new. It hadn't been out of the
garage for more than two years. I liked the Essex coach
to look at, with its plush upholstery, but there was only
room for about four people, including us. My father said
that when two people of the right class, or three people if
they were smaller, saw we were driving all the way in an
Essex coach they wouldn't hesitate to share the expenses.
Would it run? The garageman said we were free to take
it for a drive around the block. The motor turned right
over when I kicked the starter. If she smoked a little, as
she did, that was due to the long period of time she had
just sat there and not run much. I drove about a half mile
north, then came back through the park. I thought she
steered a little hard on the turns, but that might have

been because the tires were low. On the radiator cap a thermometer registered the temperature of the water, in case it got hot. She ran pretty smooth. I liked driving around in such a tight little box.

"Kid," my father said, "how you like it?"

I said I liked it fine.

My father signed the papers and gave the garageman $125 in cash. He gave us, gratis, five gallons of gas. With the free gas we took a spin through the park, the bare trees already looking pretty much like winter. There was ice building up on the pilings along the lakefront. "What are we waiting for!" my father said, and slapped his hands together. We still had four days of paid-up rent, but my father had lost his feeling that his future was in Chicago. In no way had it lived up to his expectations. If I thought about it, which I took time to do, it was Chicago that had given me the expectations that I was now looking up to—but it was easy for me, if given the chance, to shift them over to California. I would just feel stronger what I had been feeling all the time.

Coming back to a place you like can be nice, as I had felt coming back to Omaha from the farm, but taking off for California, with the first snow falling, is like nothing else.

As the motor warmed up and began to run a little loose, I could feel this dull knock through the gas pedal, even before I heard it. It more or less stopped when I gave it the gas, or we were pulling up a long grade. I'd heard that crooked car dealers would put sawdust in an engine to take up the slack and keep a bearing from knocking, but I hadn't heard what could be done about it.

Long drives nearly always made my father sleepy, and he dozed off before we reached Joliet. Near Springfield the road curved between farm buildings that sit so close to its edge I could see in the windows. Then we crossed a bridge, the water black beneath it, with a big tilted barn dark against the snow with a deep purple shadow beside it. Nothing special. Just something I would never forget.

In 1927 most of the highways led to the center of towns, then out again. When we stopped at the lights, in Springfield, the people standing on the corner could hear the loud knock of our motor. So could my father. "What's that, kid?" he said. I thought it might be a connecting rod. I didn't know what connecting rods connected, but I didn't want to mention the word "bearing." I knew about bearings. They called for a motor overhaul. When we stopped for oil my father asked the mechanic if he would like to buy a car.

"This one?" he asked.

We nodded. He listened to the knock.

"That bearing's burned out," he said.

My father said, "Make me an offer."

He put his head in to look at the plush upholstery. "Sixty dollars," he said.

My father said, "I paid more than that for the rubber."

He said, "Take it or leave it."

"Kid," my father said, "should we take it?"

"Sure," I replied.

We had supper in a café the mechanic recommended, where we sat on stools at the counter. We had lost sixty-five dollars on the deal, but my father had gone up in my estimation. He took a large supply of toothpicks from the glass when he paid the cashier.

We took a bus to St. Louis, where we saved money by taking a night bus to Kansas City. The first thing we did was go to the Kansas City *Star* and put in the same ad we had run in Chicago. As he looked through the want ads my father asked me what I thought of a 1921 Big Six Studebaker.

"How much?" I asked him.

"One sixty-five," he said.

"Not bad," I replied.

One thing it would do would be to take at least five passengers. At twenty-five dollars apiece that would almost pay for the car. Like the Essex coach, it sat at the back of a garage, but it hadn't been owned by two old ladies. The man who owned it had turned it in on a Maxwell Coupe. The tires were not so good for a trip to California, but it had a full set of side curtains.

"Should we risk it, kid?" my father asked me.

"Sure," I said.

I put the curtains on the car, and parked across the street from the hotel's steam-heated lobby. From our room at the front we could keep an eye on it. The first person we met, but not the first to sign up, was a one-legged Greek actor going to the Passion Play in Los Angeles. The part he was in was waiting for him to get there. He wore the empty leg of his pants pinned up, and spent most of the day in a chair in the lobby waiting to see if anybody signed up. He also felt he should go for less, since with just one leg he took up less room.

Mr. Griffin, from Akron, Ohio, was on his way to meet his wife, Nora, in Pasadena. He was a soft-shoe dancer, no taller than I was, wearing a checkered suit, a tight fitting cap and patent leather oxfords. He liked me all right, but he didn't get along with Mr. Dorfmann, a gambler from New Orleans, who sat and played cards with himself. We had a woman who would go as far as San Bernardino if she could ride up front with me, if I was driving, but besides two suitcases she had a roped army locker. If it turned out we didn't have a full car she could go along, but we had seven passengers. Three would sit in the front, and my father would sit on a suitcase between the foldaway seats in the rear. We put the bags in the racks on the running boards, or between the engine hood and the fenders. I'd got to be pretty friendly with the people in the lobby, but the hotel manager was glad to see us leave.

Kansas City is on a bluff overlooking the Missouri, with a pretty steep drop to the bridge, and to save the brakes on this grade I put the car in second gear to slow it. Halfway down the slope, without any warning, the whole gear box dropped right into the street. Between the legs of Mr. Griffin, who was sitting beside me, there was this big hole in the floor. Since we were on a grade I let it coast into a garage just off the road. Several people I don't remember at all took their bags off the car and just walked away. Those who didn't just sat in the car while my father made a deal to swap the Studebaker, just as it was, for a 1919 Buick touring with a California top. It was a smaller car, and not much to look at with its low hood and bicycle-size wheels, but it had an original-type

131

gearshift. Sitting there in the garage, it ran like a top. The four people left crowded the seats a bit, but they all appreciated the California top. I was so preoccupied with the gearshift I hardly got more than a glance at the Missouri, which looked about the same between the banks of snow as it did in Omaha.

About two weeks later, early in January, my father and me and a young man named Don arrived in Albuquerque, New Mexico. We still had the Buick, but none of the passengers. In the railroad station, where we passed the time and discussed with Don what we might do next, there were Indians waiting for the trains to sell their blankets and pottery. If I didn't dream it up, some of the streetcars had women motormen and conductors. It had been a long journey. I had grown accustomed to seeing strange things. Back in Gallup the one-legged actor had said goodbye to me in a bus station. Out in the street the car was buried in a foot of snow. Don had been the one who helped me get it started, and having nothing else to do had driven along with us, all of us sitting in front. He happened to be passing through Gallup at the same time we were, on his way to Long Beach from Amarillo. He showed me how to cut the bead off an old tire so it would lap around the flat tire you left on the rim and make a hard rubber tire you could ride on. He almost broke my arm when we Indian wrestled. While we were waiting for the snow to melt in the mountain passes, my father passed the time in the station lobby talking about his railroad experience with the agent. When the snow began to melt Don just rode along with us, since we had the room.

In Arizona we heard of a hole in the earth, wide and deep as a canyon, made by a falling meteor, but we couldn't see it from the road. It snowed in Flagstaff, where Don left us, and we spent the night in the warm station lobby. Near Siberia, California, or where it had once been, I didn't see the turn in the road and drove about fifty yards or more into the desert's soft sand. That's where we were, wondering what to do next, when Don came along riding a motorcycle with a sidecar. My father sat in the sidecar, and I rode on the rear of the motorcycle, holding on to Don. That's why we arrived in San Bernardino with my eyes so windburned I could hardly see it. My lips were so chapped it was painful to suck on oranges. The orange trees grew right along the road, rows and rows of them, leading back toward the mountains, some of the oranges so close we could reach out and pick them. My father had the address of a man in Cucamonga, but he was no longer living at that number, so we went on ahead, between the orange groves, the shimmering sky and the snow-capped mountains. I don't remember saying much until Azusa, where we ran out of gas.

*I*n Los Angeles we found a room off Seventh Street, in the home of a widow who was one of Aimee Semple McPherson's angels. When she was not in the temple, she was at home taking long hot baths. I had most of the day to walk up and down Main Street, looking at the watches in the pawnshop windows. On the cold rainy days I took in the shows at the Hippodrome. Sunny days I sat in the park on Olvera Street, where Sunset Boulevard ended at Main Street. George Young, who was from Canada, and hardly any older than I was, had swum from California to Catalina Island and won $25,000 of William Wrigley's money. I saw him swim in a big glass tank of water on the stage of Grauman's Chinese Theatre. Back in Chicago there was snow and slush in the streets and you could almost freeze waiting for a streetcar. Who would ever believe that I was here in California, the sun warm on my face.

Twice a day I ate the flapjacks that were cooked in a window near the Hippodrome. One day I saw the Greek actor with the one leg at a lunch counter in the Pacific Electric Car terminal on Seventh Street, but he didn't see me. My father took a position with Western Union on the strength of his experience with the Union Pacific Railroad. I could see him, in the office on Main Street, typing out telegrams to be sent as night letters, his shirt sleeves turned back to keep his cuffs clean. We planned to get a car and drive to Long Beach, where some people lived who were my second cousins and had come out here from Ohio. If it ever stopped raining I planned to get down to the ocean and take the glass-bottomed boat to Catalina. Running an errand for the widow, who paid me for it, I discovered Echo Park on West Wilshire, where there were swans on the lake and rowboats to be rented. Even my father didn't believe me when I told him I'd seen real swans on a lake in February.

One afternoon in Pershing Square I saw my father in discussion with a woman. He looked good when he was sitting and talking, with one leg crossed, his arm along the bench back, the fingers of his right hand hooked to his vest pocket. I didn't have to hear him to know he was talking about raising capital for the egg business, or this boy he had who needed a new mother. When she left he crossed the street to the Biltmore, as if he lived there, and sat in the mezzanine arcade chewing on toothpicks. It was easy to see that his pants no longer went with the coat. Although I'd meant to spy on where he was going, I changed my mind. California wasn't all he'd expected either, full of people who were tight-fisted with their money, or women who were suspicious of anybody not from Cedar Rapids. My father had been to Cedar Rapids, and if there was one town that made Omaha look pretty good, that was it.

In the streets south of Main were the used car lots, and I began to read the messages printed on the windshields. One that caught my eye was a dark green Marmon with wire wheels. On the windshield it read, SWEET RUNNER/ MAKE OFFER.

This Marmon had a Red Seal airplane motor, and a hood so long and high the driver's seat was like a cockpit. When I scrunched down in the seat the radiator cap was on my eye level, like a gunsight. There were two foldaway seats in the rear, with room to spare for some luggage. The salesman said he was from Des Moines, but he had been to Omaha with the American Legion, and seen the Ak-sar-ben parade. "Tell your daddy to make me an offer," he said. "She's a real sweet runner, with good rubber."

The good rubber was hard to see on such small wheels. I got the idea that maybe ninety dollars would buy it, if we didn't rile up the salesman. I took my father around for a look at it, and sat behind the wheel while they talked about it. My father couldn't even crank a car, but you couldn't tell him anything about them. "That car's a gas eater," he said, which was something he'd picked up somewhere. It was painful just to hear him talk about it, since I wanted it so bad it made me ache to look at it.

136

"Kid," my father said, "when he really wants to sell that car we'll be back."

Wonderful as it was in Los Angeles, compared with what it was like in Chicago, there was no lack of people who had found that California hadn't lived up to their expectations. They didn't like the natives, most of whom were from somewhere else. Others were not so keen on the climate. They missed the snow in the winter. They missed the coming of spring. We could have filled two cars with the people who wanted to leave, but not all of them could put up the money on short notice. We narrowed it down to seven, not counting the fox terrier that would ride with me in the front seat. A sailor named Red, going home to Pittsburgh, sat on one of the spares with my father. Mr. Olsen, about the size of two people, was only going as far as El Paso, where we would all have room to spare when he left. A ten-year-old boy who had an uncle in Phoenix, and was living with his aunt in Alameda at the moment, wanted to ride along with us as far as Phoenix, but experience had made my father cautious. Places on the map always looked closer than they proved to be.

No one could have asked for a sweeter-running car than that Marmon was, as far as Redlands. The sailor, Red, who was sitting on a spare, was the first to say that it sounded like valves. The hiss it made was more of a valve sound than bad plugs. Up till that moment I was inexperienced with valves, which were something an airplane motor had a lot of. When they began to seal up, as we got close to Redlands, you got a hissing effect like a

137

calliope. We got there in time to find a garage before it was dark. The two days we were there I got to know the mechanic about as well as I did the big Red Seal motor. His name was Zeke. He wore a hat he made by folding a newspaper to keep the grease out of his hair.

To make up for the time we had lost in Redlands we drove all night through the Imperial Valley but I could see better on the map how it looked. In the moonlight the Salton Sea looked black. Near Yuma the old road lay out on the sand dunes like a picket fence blown over on its side. Just out of Yuma we blew a tire and it took Mr. Olsen to pry it off the rim. Floods had washed out the bridge on the Gila River, so we had to make a detour through Indian country. It was more of a pack trail than a road, with gullies in it so deep there was a gap between the front and rear wheels. In less than half a day's driving all the tires were flat. What we did was cut the bead off the spares and just let them wrap around the rim, the way Don had showed me, or we'd still be out there somewhere. I learned later in Tucson that the Indians we saw were Papagos.

About a mile above the town we straddled the trail. Parts of it had once been a road and there was wagon room between the boulders, but now scrubs were growing at the edge and the center was bare. The foot path was smooth and dusty with donkey manure. When we knew we should have turned back there was no place to turn. It got dark while we sat and argued what we should do. Some Indians stood off a ways and looked at us. When I said "Tucson?" one of them pointed up the trail and we all felt

*better and started up again. It was soon so steep I had to
shift to low. At that speed our lights were dim and flickered like a fan was turning in front. I had to stop and race
the motor to see ahead. Coyotes were thick as cats behind
a store. Their eyes blinked at the lights and when we got
by they sat and howled, the echoes nice but the real thing
too near. There were gullies that almost stood us on end
and bent the bumper back on the fenders, and bumps I
had to squeeze around or drag the rear end. . . . The bat-
tery was running down with the lights on and I kept racing the engine like hell all the time. But she had the
power to burn, even when the hood rose up like a wall.
After a while I kind of liked it, kind of wanted bigger
gullies, liked to give her the soup and watch her climb
right out. She had enough stuff in low to climb a tree.
When it got really bad Red walked up front, his white
cap pinned to his behind . . . when the road eased off we
rolled along in second and it felt like high, which showed
how it was back where we'd just come from.* *

After we left the Papagos trading post there was no
road at all, just the downgrade slope covered with scrub
and cactus, a smudge of smoke way off to the southeast
that might be Tucson. Except for me at the wheel, everybody walked. Now and then I could see the mirrorlike
flash of sunlight on a car windshield. We came out on the
level beside an irrigation canal, with the road to Tucson
on the far side of it. Everybody took a rest, soaking their
feet in the water, then we had to go another ten miles to

*My Uncle Dudley, 1942.

139

reach a crossing. I didn't mind it so much as the others, because, as my father said, I didn't know any better. And for another thing I was driving. Tucson wasn't at all what I thought it would be, but we were able to buy good secondhand tires from a man with a machine for putting them on the rims. He didn't seem surprised to see us and wasn't at all talkative while he worked.

Clear over near Deming, in New Mexico, the threads stripped on the right front wheel; when it dropped off I could see it for a moment at the rim of the lights. We had to wait till daylight to find it in the desert, then spend half the morning jacking up the front end. Crossing Texas there were days we made as much as 150 miles. It was cold driving at night, but warmed up fine during the day. Windburn alone gave me a good tan, and I often had the sun on my face in the morning. I especially liked the country around Shreveport, Louisiana, where the shacks back in the woods were like cans of Log Cabin syrup. The colored people hadn't seen many cars like ours, and most of them waved.

Just before noon we rolled into Lake Village, Arkansas. There was a lake with a pier at the foot of the street, but it was no resort. The road just ended there, facing the water, so I had to turn around and go back to the tracks. Crossing the tracks, which I did real easy, I felt this thump like the wheels had dropped off in the rear. When Red got out to check the wheels they were still there, but the rear-end transmission had dropped right on the tracks. I could tell that the two or three colored people who came closer to look at us thought we were crazy. We'd been driving all night, and with Mr. Olsen gone there was room enough to sleep in the back seat. It was so warm flies buzzed around us, but nobody moved. My father sat on one of the spares, his head resting on the back of the front seat. Red walked around to the back side of the car and peed on one of the wheels. They had a general store, and a feed store with this hand-cranked gas pump, but no garage. I was so tired I just sat there at the wheel as if waiting for a train to hit us. In the quiet I could hear the far-off pealing of bells.

"Maybe they just heard the war's ended," said Red, and guffawed.

A flat wagon, hitched to some sleepy mules, came down the street toward us, then turned at the corner. Packed tight on the tailboard, their legs dangling, were five or six colored boys, one holding a puppy. They didn't holler or wave, they just sat there. A white man, wearing an apron, came out of the general store, put two fingers in his mouth, shrilly whistled. All my life I had tried to do that, and couldn't. Both Red and me looked at him with admiration. Red said to him, "What happened?"

"Levee broke," he replied, and went back inside.

Everything he owned Red left in the duffel bag on the running board. "Let's go, kid," he said to me, and I climbed over the door, forgetting all sorts of stuff I meant to remember under the front seat. We were both good runners and caught up with the wagon, but it was moving so slow we went right by it. Up ahead of us, where the road forked, we could see people strung along carrying sacks and parcels. I could see that what I'd needed all these weeks was a good long run. We passed a lot of people, all of them friendly, to where the road ended at a pier. An excursion type boat, with a canvas awning, was taking on people. They still had room when we took off, but it seemed so calm and peaceful I didn't worry. There was hardly a ripple on the water until we got to where we could see it moiling. It was more like a lake than a river but we could see by the shore how fast we were drifting. I didn't really understand what a levee was, or what it would mean to have a break in it, until we got out of the boat near Greenville and I saw the whole city in the hollow below us, the river maybe thirty feet or more above it. Except for the queasy feeling that it gave me, it was a nice warm, balmy spring day.

Once we got across the river I could see that Red didn't want me tagging along behind him. Two people made it harder to catch a ride. He said I should look him up when I got to Pittsburgh, and gave me his home address and two dollars. I was on my own.

I spent the night in the Greenville depot, waiting for the levee to break and the river to wash us all away. The station was crowded with people looking for their friends and relations. I thought I might find my father, since he felt more at home in a railroad station than anywhere else. I didn't see him, nor did I see Mr. Hansen, a big Swede I had grown to like. The fact was, except for Red and my father, I wasn't sure how many of us had arrived at the river. We had been so long crossing Texas I had lost track of both time and people.

In the early morning, on the road going north, a traveling salesman in a Maxwell coupe took me almost as far as Memphis. If I hadn't minded making all of the stops I could have ridden with him farther. He called the colored

142

people in the cotton fields on both sides of the road a lot of niggers. He didn't mean it bad. He liked most of them. It was very exceptional, he told me, to see a white boy like me walking along the road in Mississippi. I said that I was headed for Chicago, but not that I'd come all the way from California. If I'd told him that he wouldn't have believed me. For all their traveling, the salesmen I met hadn't seen as much of the world as I had.

There was a lot of flooding around Cairo, but it was easy to hitch a ride to St. Louis. Until they heard me talk, most people thought I was a victim of the flood, looking for my relations. In the St. Louis bus station, where I spent the night, I got to talking with one of the drivers. He said if I would stand on the corner he told me, he might pick me up, then again he might not. It all depended. But there was a chance he might. I was there on the spot he told me, and that's how I got a free ride from St. Louis to the Loop in Chicago, my hometown.

It was still only April, but a warm drizzle made it seem like summer, the streets slick and sticky. I just walked around and around in the Loop, feeling good to be back. I had a piece of pie at Pixley & Ehlers, where you can see people making them through the window, then I took a Clark streetcar to Menominee. It was like they all said, there's nothing like spring in Lincoln Park. A team with uniforms was holding a baseball practice on one of the diamonds that was not too muddy, and I could see the batter hit the ball before I heard the crack.

My father had arrived two days before I did, but he was still in bed catching up on his sleep. While he fried some eggs he told me of his plans to get back into the egg business. Until he raised the capital, what he would do would be to work nights for the railroad, sorting waybills. Would I like to know what he had learned? I said I would. Kid, he said, take my word, the grass isn't greener on the other side of the road.

At the Y Mr. Shults was glad to see me and offered me the job I had had in the lobby, but the truth was I no longer felt like working with kids. I did help him with the Bible Club on Sunday, where I gave them a talk about my trip to California, but seeing the world had given me ideas. I forget what they were, but almost everywhere I looked the grass looked as green as Christmas jewelry.

I took a job as office boy in the insurance department of the Commonwealth Edison Company in the Loop. My job was to air out the office in the morning, adjust all the blinds, and stamp and seal a lot of letters. I also carried checks that had to be signed to Mr. Samuel Insull's office on the floor above. He was a small, quiet man who didn't say much, and looked pretty dried up. I'd seen people like him in California. On those days there were not so many letters to stamp I got in a lot of drawing practice.

If I was offered something big with Commonwealth Edison I would stay with them, and save my money, otherwise I looked forward to being with my friends at Lakeview High School. We didn't horse around so much as we used to, but talked a lot about what we planned to do. Gene Logsdon was dating some girl named Florence, so we hardly saw him on weekends. What I planned to do, and right away, was build myself up. I had grown two inches in about five months, but I was stringy as pulled taffy. Traveling around with grown men, I took a lot of kidding I wouldn't have taken if I had had more muscle. In the window of a drugstore on LaSalle Street, I saw a man with a build like Lionel Strongfort exercising with a strip of rubber. He could make every muscle in his chest ripple with it. I didn't believe everything that I saw or read, but it was less than a dollar, with instructions, so I bought it. Just before I went to bed I exercised for half an hour, and drank a pint of milk along with a cake of Fleischmann's yeast. It took some doing to get the yeast down, but chocolate milk helped. I couldn't believe it myself when I went to the Y and saw how I looked in the locker-room mirror. I'd gained more than four pounds in about three weeks. On the strength of that I exercised in the morning for at least twenty minutes before I went to work, and I used a spring-grip exerciser when I was walking around or riding the streetcars. I drank an awful lot of milk. Eddie Kovack, the Y phys ed instructor, saw me doing exercises on the parallel bars. I could see he couldn't believe it. "What's going on here?" he said, feeling my triceps. It wasn't hard for me to keep at anything that worked. I got permission to pull the weights at the Y on Sundays, after I had finished with the Bible Club.

My boss at work, Charlie Miller, who came to work in his slippers because he had foot problems, had a talk with me about my future. He had hired me because we were both farmboys, and he felt I had a future in the department. But I let my mind wander. He could see that from where he sat. It had pleased him to take me into the department, and he had no serious complaints about my work, but increasingly he felt that I was not really there in the office with the rest of them. Not 100 percent. So where was I? I liked Charlie Miller, but I couldn't tell him that what I had on my mind was grass so green I could almost eat it. I saw it everywhere I looked. I said I really didn't know where I was, because I'd already been to so many places, like Omaha, Kansas City, Albuquerque, Yuma, Los Angeles, El Paso, Shreveport, Louisiana, and Lake Village, Arkansas, in the flood, but I knew all right.

One day in May Charlie Miller held my legs at the window of his office while I emptied all of our wastebaskets on Lindbergh, the Lone Eagle, below on Clark Street. If there was one thing Lindbergh knew, Charlie Miller said, it was where he was. And where he was going.

My father agreed to pay me ten dollars a week over the summer if I would help him sort his waybills at night. That way we would both have most of the daytime free. I'd come to work about midnight, when the tower room was cooler, and usually work until about daylight. I liked being in the tower, but I hated the work. Handling the carbon sheets of waybills blackened my fingers, and I picked up splinters from the edge of the sorting table. I didn't like the way my father, so he could sort the bills better, always flicked his dirty thumb on his tongue, leaving a raw-looking pink spot. He worked in his shirt sleeves, the cuffs turned back, but leaning over the table frayed the material at the front of his pants. He was getting a pot, like Mr. Miller, and after working for an hour he had to rest and get off his feet. From the tower room we could see the traffic flowing over the drawbridge, and watch it go up like a wall when a boat passed. High at the top of the span the lights blinked like planets. Behind it the lights of cars glowed like a fire at an oven door. Two or three times an hour my father would pause to look at the clock on the Wrigley Tower.

"What time is it, kid?" he would ask me, but he never remembered what I told him. He didn't wear his own watch because it made a bulge in his pants where he leaned on the table. Some nights we were still there when the sky lit up in the east.

When my father took the job, and the weather was good, he liked to walk down Chicago Avenue to the waterworks, then along Michigan Boulevard and the Gold Coast to Lincoln Park. But that summer his feet were so tired after standing all night he would take a streetcar to Clark Street and transfer. The cars ran so seldom at that time in the morning he had time to get his breakfast at a Thompson's restaurant between transfers. I might see him sitting in the Thompson's when I passed by. On the hot summer nights there would still be people on the beach at Oak Street sleeping on the sand. Before I reached Lincoln Park there might be lights on in the windows of the top-floor apartments and rich people with their horses on the bridle path. On a walk that long I must have done a lot of thinking, but if I did I've forgotten what it was.

If the old man who sorted waybills in the freight yards felt himself more alive there than anywhere else, it had something to do with the tower room where he worked. On one

147

side of the room was a large bay window that faced the east. A man standing at this window—like the man on the canal who let the drawbridge up and down—felt himself in charge of the flow of traffic, of the city itself. All that he saw seemed to be in his province, under his control. He stood above the sprawling freight yards, the sluggish canal, the three or four bridges that sometimes crossed it, and he could look beyond all of these things, beyond the city itself, to the lake. He couldn't see this lake, of course, but he knew it was there. And when the window stood open he could detect the smell of it . . . In the windows along the canal the blinds were usually drawn, and behind the blinds, when the lights came on, he could see the people moving around. Nearly all of them ate at the back of the house, then moved to the front. There they would talk, or sit and play cards, or wander about from room to room until it was time, as the saying goes, to go to bed. Then the front lights would go off, other lights come on. A woman would stand facing the mirror, and a man, scratching himself, would sit on the edge of the sagging bed, holding one shoe, peering into it as if his foot was still there. Or letting it fall so that it was heard in the room below . . . In all of this there was nothing unusual—every night it happened everywhere—except that the people in these rooms were not alone. The old man in the tower room, the waybills in his hand, was there with them. He had his meals with them in the back, then wandered with all of them to the front, listened to the talk, and then saw by his watch it was time to go to bed. He sat there on the edge, looking at his feet or the hole in the rug.*

* *The Works of Love.*

148

In the fall I went back to school and did the cartoons for the school newspaper. I saw my old school friends on weekends, when we either took in a movie or listened to the New York Philharmonic on Mrs. Johnson's new console radio. To get it into the front room the player piano had to be moved out. We listened to Wayne King, at the Aragon Ballroom, and I first heard Johann Sebastian Bach's Air for the G String on it. I bought a ukulele, and worked especially hard on "Little White Lies."

In my English class I sat across from a girl who wore a Red Cross Life Saving pin on her sweater. I, too, was a Red Cross Life Saver; I wore the pin on the lapel of my blue serge suit. In Dorothy's excitement to answer a question, her arms waving, the bone pins often fell from her hair, which I retrieved. The bone hairpins between her teeth, her arms raised to rearrange her hair, the downward gaze of her eyes left me free to be ravished by the beauty of this gesture. In the curve of her arms a halo crowned her light brown hair. Dry-mouthed, I put a tongue to my chapped lips. I did not lack images for my condition, but an occasion for adoration. In the hallways and on the stairs I plotted ways to approach her. She usually hugged four or five books to her front, an apple perched on the top. I would appear at her side and say, "Gee, I wish I was one of those books!" I planned to do so many things I am no longer sure what it was I did. The startled glance of pleasure she gave me I remember. Strands of her light brown hair framed her face. I did not have the words, but I was at ease in a landscape appropriate to my emotions. Sir Gawain and the Green Knight were my close companions. I approached the dark tower several times daily. Soon I was carrying her books the eight or ten blocks to the elevated stop where we parted. In a swoon of emotion I returned to the Y where the facts of life were my supporting fiction. I shouted in the lobby, prayed better than ever, divvied up the loot of the slot machine raids, and exercised for at least half an hour on the parallel bars after the lobby closed. Back in the room on Menominee Street I gulped down a cake of Fleischmann's yeast, and washed fig newtons down with chocolate milk, to increase my weight. In the early morning, as the school doors opened, I was there in the hall with the pounding radiators, my homework assignments, and the plaster statue of Joan of Arc with the hole in her ear where marbles were inserted.

I might see my girl, a wild exchange of glances, when she made a brief stop at her locker to pick up a book or fuss with her hair. Under pressure my father went with me into the Loop, where I could try on hats in a men's hat store. I saw my small pale face in the large three-way mirrors. I compensated by choosing a large man-size Stetson with a rolled brim, like my father's.

"Better it's a little big," said the clerk. "Give him time to grow into it."

Had he noted that I was growing in other departments? My father's coats fit me in the chest but were long in the sleeves. To show off my new muscles I took my girl to the beach where she disliked the sand and feared the water. A towel tucked about her plump knees and wide bottom, she wore a straw hat to keep the sun off her face. She did not swim a stroke. The Red Cross Life Saving pin she had acquired, in a swap of pins, from a friend who didn't swim a stroke either. Nevertheless, I was the first person to slip my hands inside of her rain-coat, and she was the first to kiss, and put cold cream on, my chapped lips. She was far and away the best friend this boy had ever had.

On Sundays I rode the streetcar for two hours to where she lived, then we rode for another two hours to the movie. Back at her place we sat in the dark of the stairs where I developed a line of talk that was more than prayer. Her father played the organ in a movie on Clark Street, where he led the singing during the intermission. I saw him only in the dark. He pretended not to see us, rattling his keys. With the taste of her face powder still on my lips I would run the four blocks to the end of the car line, where the conductor might be changing the trolley, or walking through the car to switch the seats to face the other direction. I often had the long rocking, clattering ride all to myself.

I had proved my talents for prayer at the Y. Now I learned the art of fiction and self-promotion. Tirelessly and silently she listened to my weekly adventure serial. What did I say? I remember nothing. My life and great times had filled me with impressions, and I planned to be a political cartoonist, like John T. McCutcheon of the Chicago *Tribune.* The one of his I liked the best showed a boy daydreaming in the twilight of an Indian summer day, where he thought he saw Indian wigwams where there were only shocks of corn. I, too, was given to seeing things where there was little to see, or to seeing them as other than what they were. Seeing a picture of my girl, her blue eyes tinted, a wash of color over a blur of freckles, my father turned back to brushing his hair in the mirror. "You can't go wrong with her, kid," he said, as if it had ever crossed my mind. I resented the suggestion, but occasionally wondered what it might be like.

She loved music, and was a voice in the throng in the school production of Schubert's *Rosamunde*. Her love of music had come from her father. At one time he had had his own orchestra and played the solo violin under the spotlight. But with the new sound movies, all the theaters needed was the organ playing when the movie was over. I don't think he liked me, but the only time he saw me was in the dark.

On the streetcar one Sunday night, Dorothy and I heard this loud guffawing right behind us. It was my father, with one of his men friends from the office. They were laughing at us. My father was still a pretty good-looking man when you saw him dressed up. He was wearing a hat so much like mine we probably looked like a vaudeville act or something. I didn't let on that I knew him from Adam, or the hick with him, who had a boil on his neck that was healing, but I knew that my ears were burning. It ruined the evening for me, for both of us, and when I couldn't explain what was wrong with me she said I didn't like her as much as I used to. The moment she said it I knew that I didn't, and it increased my shame. I lied and said that I really liked her better than ever, which had the effect of making me moody. On the long ride home I saw my reflection in the window, the big hat tilted on my head, and that I looked like a fool. I took the hat off, put in on the seat beside me, and left it there when I got off. It was like new, that hat, the band stamped with my initials, but I could no more wear it after what had happened than I could a dunce cap, or a nightpot. I was so full of pity for myself, my throat aching, I rode past Menominee clear to Division Street, from where, since there were no more cars running, I had to walk back.

One thing that I stuck with, because it worked, was my exercise program. After the Y lobby had closed in the evening I would get in a workout on the parallel bars. In my zeal to be Lionel Strongfort I would come over on Sunday for an extra session. Yeast, milk and fig newtons were transformed into muscles overnight. Beneath the calluses on the palm of my right hand I noticed, and ignored, a point of soreness. It did not go away. And I did not stop my workouts. Soon I was hardly able to make a fist, and the skin on the back of my hand was puffy. One Saturday morning I spoke to my father, showing him my hand. He thought it was just a bruise that would heal, but we went together into the Loop to see the railroad doctor in the station. A big gruff man with a lame walk, he asked me what I had been doing to get such calluses. I told him. I think we better take a look inside, he said, and led me to the sink. He asked my father to grip my wrist while he turned the palm up, just to look at it. Tell me where it feels a little sore, he said, touching it with a knife blade, as if all he meant to do was prick it. He was quick. I watched the ribbon of black blood ooze from the cut, thickened with the creamy cloud of pus. Just what I thought, he said, and set me on a stool so I could hold my hand in a bowl of hot water. I had to soak it forever, until it looked parboiled, then he wrapped it in a bandage saturated with a solution that would shrink the flesh. In two days I would come back and see him.

I spent Sunday with Dorothy, who showed great concern, and when the doctor saw me on Monday morning he said, "Well, that looks a little better. I guess we'll just let you keep it, not chop it off." He joshed me, but I knew that he meant it. At night, the hand beside me on a pillow, I pondered how it must feel to have one missing. I visualized it with other missing hands, in a bucket. On a visit to a class at the Y college I had caught a glimpse of a dismembered cadaver. I lacked the nerve to think about such matters, and accepted them as unthinkable subjects. When my hand was removed from the shrinking solution it was not my hand, but like that of a mummy. If the fingers touched each other it was like an electric shock.

During this time Dorothy copied out my school assignments, and held my hand like a bird when we rode on the streetcar. It shamed me to think that my love had been so weak, and I wondered what it would be like to be married. If she was my wife, perhaps my love would grow strong again. But Dorothy planned to go to Northwestern, where she would study music, and I was working for fifteen dollars a week in the cloakroom at the Y. The Y itself had changed, with open houses on weekends, and girls using the pool and the locker rooms. As strange as it seems, the water in the pool had a different smell and taste after the girls had used it. Some of them refused to soap when they used the showers. They had dances in the gym on Saturday nights, with some of the girls smoking in the lobby, and it was no surprise to me when Mr. Shults took on a brand-new Y in Sheboygan, Wisconsin. He said he would make a place for me as soon as I had finished school. But it was Dorothy's opinion, and I suppose it was mine, that anyone as smart as I was owed it to himself to go on to college. But the only college open to me, besides the Y, was the City College of Chicago, on the South Side. I had never even heard of it until she told me about it. There was no tuition. All you had to do was supply your own books. It wasn't my idea of college, once I got a look at it, a big barn of a building, like a department store, with a basketball team nobody ever heard of. One of my friends, Bill Miller, planned to be a streetcar conductor, his father knowing people in the department; Orville Clark was going to Purdue to become an engineer; and Maurie Johnson could go to work the day school was over in his father's dairy. Emmanuel Guagliardo was already making more than I was, driving a pie truck. As talented as I was, I considered myself not very talented. What I could do was apply myself, as I did to drawing and exercising, but no amount of exercising was going to make me into Lionel Strongfort. I had gone with my drawings down to the *Daily News* and looked through the smoky office for the cartoonist, who didn't look at all like an artist when somebody pointed him out. He had his sleeves rolled and his shirttails were out of his pants. When my father looked at the want ads in the *Tribune* some of them always seemed to have him in mind, but when I looked at the ads all they ever wanted was BOYS. I was no longer a boy. What I was was not clear.

While I was pondering my future I received a parcel from a man in Texas, D. V. Osborn, who claimed to be my mother's brother and my uncle. In a hand like my father's, the point of the pencil put to his lips to wet it, he said he wanted me to read the book he had sent me to make sure I didn't follow a religious calling, like other members of the family. The book he sent me was *Elmer Gantry,* by Sinclair Lewis. I had never read anything like it. D. V. Osborn told me that if I was strong and willing to work, he would offer me a job running a tractor on his ranch. He would pay me thirty dollars a month and my keep. If at the end of the year he had a big crop, which was not unlikely, he would pay me another 20 percent, which might come to as much as six or seven thousand dollars. With that I could do pretty much as I wanted. But I shouldn't give a thought to any of it if I didn't like to work.

I knew nothing of my mother's side of the family but her name, Ethel Grace Osborn. I had the name Wright Marion from my grandfather, but I knew nothing of D. V. Osborn. The novel he sent me opened my eyes. I liked it better than those of Alexander Dumas and Walter Scott. The thought of riding around on a tractor pleased me, but I didn't believe, as I explained it to Dorothy, that I would ever get a lot of money for it. What I would get, if I worked hard enough, would be thirty dollars a month. I wrote my uncle to thank him for the book, which I liked, and to assure him that I was not at the moment contemplating a religious calling. What puzzled me was why he should think I might be. He didn't know about the talent I had for prayer, or anything like that. Mr. Shults would have said, when he got to know me, that I was pretty much open to a religious calling, but not in the church. Christian service did seem to appeal to me in those areas where I was good at it, counseling the Friendly Indians, divvying up their swag, and talking to them at camp with the lights out. I could sure use seven thousand dollars, I wrote him, since I was about to enter college, but I couldn't afford to gamble on it while I was making thirty dollars a month. If he really was my uncle and my mother's brother I thought sure he would make me another proposition—but he didn't. He didn't answer my letter, or even send me another book.

Right at the last minute Dorothy decided she would go to City College along with me. She said she didn't feel that we should be parted, but what she really wanted to do was keep her eye on me. City College was jam-packed with girls who were a lot more forward than those at Lakeview. They were also brighter. That was also true of the boys. I had never had to compete with Jewish boys before, and they ran circles around me. Dorothy had more time to study than I did, and filled me in while we were riding on the streetcars, but I was getting C's in the history of art, where I was smart. I tried to catch up on my sleep in the study periods. In late November, flushed with a fever and the need to write a paper on Charles Martel, I sat at a table in the library where college pamphlets were available. I leafed through several, then began to read about Pomona College, in California. I had almost been there. It had been along the route, edging the foothills, my father and I had passed through on the motorcycle. At the front of the pamphlet a photograph showed the orange groves and the snow-capped mountains. The text described the details that were missing: groves of oranges, the scent of blossoming trees, shimmering sunlight on snow-capped mountains, a land without winter where boys and girls strolled about with their books in an eternal summer, tanned by the sun.

On my fevered imagination this had the effect of a vision. After all, I had been there. I was a true believer. This word image of the cloudland on the horizon met all the requirements of my extravagant dreaming. Did I thieve this pamphlet, or just the picture? Or did I really have need of either? In the thralldom of this vision I made my way home to the bed just vacated by my father. A week passed, and I was still in it, one of the fortunate survivors of that winter's flu epidemic. In the mailbox, where my father seldom troubled to look, I found a letter, forwarded from Texas, from my mother's sister Winona, in Boise, Idaho. She wanted to tell me that they all loved me, that I was one of the family, and that my grandfather was willing to pay my expenses if I would attend one of the Seventh-Day Adventist colleges. One of these colleges was in the mountains north of San Francisco. On my way to this college, if I decided to attend it, I would stop off in Boise, Idaho, and visit with my mother's people.

Was not this an example of divine intervention?

My father thought it might be, but he felt it was long overdue. He recalled that my grandfather, before I was born, had lost a fortune in land in the Galveston flood, and later owned property in Canada. By rights I was one of his heirs. Who knew what he owned in Idaho? The thought of my inheritance spurred my father to take a fresh look at the egg business.

I hastened to write my Aunt Winona that I accepted my grandfather's offer, but I did not think it advisable to explain that I was not looking forward to a religious calling. I had never heard of the Seventh-Day Adventists. What appealed to me, and seemed divinely inspired, was that this college was in California. In one way or another I had to get there. I would appear in Boise, Idaho, as soon as I received the railroad ticket.

With sad eyes Dorothy heard this story as she studied my reflection in the streetcar window. I was wearing one of my father's old topcoats. I was wan and pale-faced, but buoyant with optimism. She saw and feared the worst. What inspired me was *flight.*

On a fiber footlocker on loan from Orville Clark, I pasted the pennants of the Big Ten colleges and others. I returned to City College to impress my history teacher with this turn in my fortunes. She had not heard of Pacific Union College. Had I finished my paper on Charles Martel? I had worked very hard to impress this woman whose mocking smile both challenged and disturbed me. While I stood waiting to be reassured she turned from me to erase the blackboard. It did not occur to me at the time, but I think she resented losing a convert. She liked boys who were both anxious and hard to please, like me.

My last night in Chicago, Dorothy and I went to see the four Marx brothers in *The Cocoanuts.* Later she cried, and we clung together in the dark stairwell smelling of wet galoshes, but fifty years would pass before I could measure my real loss against my imaginary gain.

𝒯wo of my mother's sisters, Winona and Violet, with Violet's husband, met me at the station in Boise. It was so dark I saw little of their faces. We drove through the snow to a farm in the country where my grandfather lived with Violet and her husband. In the lamplight at the supper table I first saw their smiling ruddy faces. It was explained to the old man that I was the son of Grace. He looked at me with wonder, his pale eyes blinking. He was subject to spells of absent-minded confusion and might stay in the barn with the cattle, or attempt to hitch himself to a plow or a wagon. He drew me to him to look at me closely, his hands firmly gripping my shoulders. He remembered my mother but he seemed to have forgotten she had had a son. I could see in the looks they gave me that they all doubted my existence until they saw me, and

I saw them. The sisters were agreed that I resembled my mother. That I had come to them in the Christmas season was a gift from God and a revelation. Their love and interest in me loosened my tongue. I told them about my travels and adventures, but I did not say much about my father. Why had he not kept in touch with my mother's people? Seated around the table to which four leaves had been added were the parts of my life that had proved to be missing. My impression of them all—the old man already dozing, the sisters with their open, affectionate faces, the warmth I felt to be accepted as one of their number—restored to my mind an image of the good life that I had once glimpsed and put behind me.

Later I shared a large bed with two of the men, one of them Marion's husband, and in the hushed darkness, the fire crackling, he explained that if I did not find the college what I had expected I need not feel bound to stay there. They would understand. In their interest in me, in their loving remembrance, after all these years, of my mother, they were unlike any people I had ever met. Meeting them provided me with an image of human goodness that I had been lacking, and I sensed that it need not be good for me to be good in itself.

In the morning, from Marion, I learned that my Aunt Winona had once had a beau and planned to marry, but on the ride to the train her husband told me that although Winona was a remarkable woman, no man would take the place of Jesus in her affections, unless it was me. My mother had been her favorite sister, and she had waited all these years to meet me. He doubted that my mother could love me with such purity of heart.

No one had ever spoken to me in this manner of the purity of love. My eyes brimmed with tears, knowing in my heart how unworthy of such love I was. I saw her briefly at the station, her hands in a fur muff, snow sparkling in her hair when she leaned forward to kiss me, my heart almost bursting with the knowledge of my own losses. My own mother would have spoiled me, and deep in my soul I longed to be spoiled.

On the station platform at St. Helena, California, I met Mr. Kirby, a barber from Los Angeles and a dead ringer for Calvin Coolidge. A recent convert to the Adventist faith, he was on his way to enter the college at Angwin. Kirby was short and slight, deliberate in his manner, dignified. I marveled that a grown man would be entering a college. We were taken by car into the mountains where the wooden buildings of the campus sat under towering trees on the rim of a meadow. Since we had arrived together, and had no objection, we shared the same room. Steam heat crackled in the radiator. Several inches of snow bordered the paths between the buildings. That was not my idea of California but I was told it was unusual. The winters were cool, with considerable rain, but it seldom snowed.

Friendly young men came to our door to greet us and explain the rules of the dormitory. There was a curfew at nine-thirty, when the lights were put out. In the morning at seven we came together for prayers, then proceeded to the dining hall between the men's and women's dormitories. My friend Kirby greatly impressed me with his gallant behavior with the ladies, something that he had learned as a barber. He assisted with their chairs at the table. He passed them food before serving himself. During this first meal I learned that those of Adventist faith did not eat meat. A meatlike preparation, made of nuts, carrots and raisins, remained on our plates at dinner. Kirby assured me it would take a bit of getting used to. In Los Angeles he had frequently sampled similar food in a health cafeteria. His own health good, he had not required it.

Kirby was a devoted reader of the Bible, but not in the manner that I read it. What he read he took to be a fact. The whole bit about the Ark, with the animals in pairs, and Jonah swallowed by the whale, he accepted as history. He saw Jesus walking on the water. I had heard there were people like that but until I met Kirby I had not known one. In the way he liked girls he was pretty normal. Soon enough I found out that all of the readers in our dormitory were like Kirby. It was news to them that there were also readers like me. At the Y, I had become a staunch supporter of Jesus, who took on, and defeated, the forces of evil, but I was pretty skimpy in matters of doctrine. The first book I bought was a leather-bound Bible with two ribbon markers to keep my place. On the flyleaf I put my name, my high school, and after considerable thought I put my address as Chicago, Illinois, U.S.A.

Every night of the week, once the lights were out, boys gathered in our room for a discussion. Some of them brought along flashlights they beamed on the ceiling. Kirby sat on a chair, being the oldest, but the rest of us sat around on the floor. I just naturally assumed that when they all knew better they would be reading the Bible my way. First I explained how it took more than six days to create the world. In the Field Museum in Chicago I had seen fossils of creatures so huge they had become extinct, thousands of years ago. And that was nowhere near the beginning. I had also heard about mastodons preserved in Siberian ice. With my own eyes I had seen petrified trees that had grown where there was now nothing but desert. How did I know that? I had read it, and believed what I had read. They really crowed to hear me talk like that, and then assured me that what I had read had been lies. The word of God was written down in the Bible, and I could read it myself.

I didn't believe that for a moment, but night after night, as we sat and talked, and as I began to make converts, it crossed my mind that I didn't know much more than they did. We believed what we had read, and we had read different books. In the Book of Genesis were the boasts of a braggart to impress his listeners, not unlike myself. The pleasure it gave me to hold their attention was like that of a prophet speaking to his disciples. I was no prophet, but they were sure good listeners. They all carried what I had said to their classes, and I was soon advised by the Dean in a very friendly and considerate manner that my own faith was my own business, but while I was a student at the college I should not try to convert others. Kirby agreed with that, since he felt his own faith was crumbling. There were trees in California which were older than the Bible's story of creation. If God could be wrong about details like that, He had probably slipped on some others.

I gave the Dean my word of honor there would be no more discussions after the lights were out. I couldn't stop what had been started, however, and most of the time

Kirby and me sat alone at our table in the dining room. Only agnostics dared to sit with us. Kirby turned for consolation to the older girls who liked to take walks in the woods on weekends, and walking around the campus by myself was how I stumbled on the gymnasium. No one had mentioned they had a basketball court, and three almost new balls. The building was pretty dark, and on the cool side, but with a floor so waxed it looked new. I played for about an hour by myself, running up and down, shooting baskets. The next day I brought Kirby along with me, but he was not the athletic type. If I flipped the ball to him it might hit him in the face, as if he didn't see it. He liked to watch me, and chase balls for me, but I soon got tired of that. Here we had a real gym, with balls to play with, and nobody playing. I brought the matter up with some boys in our dorm who seemed to know what a basketball was. They didn't know much, but they liked to play. One of the problems was they had to play in their socks on a slippery waxed floor. It was comical to see them skidding around, but they scrambled for the ball like crazy. They hollered and yelled like girls. To make it more fun, and introduce a little order, I organized them into two teams of four players each. I'd never seen grown kids get so excited. They didn't know how to shoot baskets or really dribble, so that a high-scoring game might be about six points. But since they had no idea how awful they were, they had a lot of fun.

After three or four days we had about twenty kids, which was enough for four teams, with five on a team, but not one of them let out a peep about the rule against games. The reason the gym had been sitting there empty was that any sort of competition was forbidden. You could come in and bounce the ball around, the way I did, but you couldn't take sides and play a game to win. They kept that secret to themselves because they were out of their minds to play. Skidding around in their socks on the slippery floor, they often fell down and got a lot of floor burns. Little they cared. As the competition warmed up we began to have some fights under the basket. One boy had a finger poked into his eye. There wasn't a game we didn't have several nosebleeds. The scrapping didn't always stop in the gym but began in earnest back in the dorms. One night we had a row, with pillow feathers strewn up and down the halls. One of the smaller boys was tied up like a bandit and locked in a closet. I had nothing to do with any of this, but when the Dean looked into it my name was mentioned. I had been the one to organize them all into teams. All of that was acceptable where I had come from, but it was not acceptable at the college. The Dean was grateful for what had happened, however, since it dramatized the evils of competition. I could see that myself. When boys got excited and played to win they were soon indifferent to the pain they gave to others. Others got pleasure in striking one another. The Dean was fond of me, and I liked him, but since my arrival I had brought nothing but disorder and confusion to the students in the dormitory. For the sake of the college he would have to ask me to leave. He would write to my people, however, that this was in no way a reflection on my character, but stemmed from the fact that I had lacked an Adventist upbringing. The opinions I had voiced to him and others were surely made in good faith, and my own, but they were contrary to Adventist doctrine and created an intolerable confusion. He found it hard to believe that I had been one of their students just under four weeks.

When I was asked to leave the school, I didn't want to. A budding evangelist myself, perhaps I enjoyed making converts. Here at the college my audience was captive. Their ignorance, on the average, was greater than my own. I could look forward—if left to my own persuasions—to modifying the nature of Adventist doctrine. The doctrine could also look forward, as I had told the Dean, to modifying me. There was something to be said for non-competition, and I might be the one to say it.

The Dean was pleased to hear that, and his mind was not closed to possible changes in my own doctrines, but for the time being he felt sure that I would make faster progress elsewhere. From my Aunt Winona I had a loving letter assuring me that what I had done was God's decision, and their love went with me in my intention to go to work for my Uncle Dwight in Texas. I had learned from Winona that Dwight was her favorite brother. I also wrote to him that I was on my way, and that I looked forward to word from him, and a month's advance pay, care of General Delivery, Los Angeles. I believe that my friend Kirby would have left with me, but he had become attached to a plump young woman from Glendale who waited on tables. While in Los Angeles he recommended I should visit his former barber shop, mention his name and get a cut-rate haircut.

After paying my coach fare to Los Angeles I still had about twenty dollars in cash. I felt so sure I would soon hear from my Uncle Dwight that I took a room in the YMCA on Hope Street. From the fire escape on the ninth floor I could see the lights, sparkling like stars, to the black rim of the sea at Long Beach. Nothing I had previously seen so far exceeded my expectations. Just three years before I had been in Los Angeles with my father, and I knew my way around, as well as most of the movies and pawnshops on Main Street. I rode the double-decker buses out to Echo Lake Park and watched the people feed bread to the swans and the goldfish. On those days it rained I went to a movie. I ate when I was hungry. Every day I took the long walk to the post office near Olvera Street, where I expected a letter from my uncle. I got to be friendly with the General Delivery clerk, who was from Akron, Ohio, and new to the city like I was. On the weekend, with the PO closed, I rode one of the Big Red cars of the Pacific Electric Railroad out to Claremont, the home of Pomona College. I walked around on the campus like I was a student, saying hi to the suntanned boys and girls. What it all made me think of was the Garden of Eden with oranges growing on the trees of knowledge. The snow-capped mountains looked so near I could touch them. On the football field I sat in the bleachers watching the shadows rise on the foothills. Nothing more beautiful could be imagined. I was dazzled with anticipation. It also seemed implausible to me that I should be deprived of something I craved so profoundly. One thing I would do would be to write my Aunt Winona that I had found the school that I wanted. Surely they would make it possible for me to attend it. If it had been a weekday, and the college offices open, I would have introduced myself to the Dean as a prospective student from Chicago, with relations who lived in Hereford, Texas, and Boise, Idaho.

I spent the night in one of the ivy-covered buildings

with windows that framed the snow-capped mountains. With dawn I was still buoyant, mingling with the students in the hallways, and I presented myself at the office of the person in charge of admissions. Perhaps he sensed it was idle to calm me. He allowed that a young man from Chicago might have something to contribute to the college. I had read, and agreed with, sentiments carved in stone on the college gates. Still buoyant, my future determined, I took the Big Red car back to the city, where I found a postcard from my uncle in Texas. He was pleased to learn that I had left a school that taught nothing but lies and falsehoods, but he was not accustomed to paying his hired hands in advance. If I was to work for him, he urged me to arrive as soon as possible, or it would be too late. The spring plowing had started. His wife, Agnes, was now taking my place on the tractor.

I found I was short the bus fare to Texas by three dollars. The PO clerk loaned me a dollar, and I pawned the silver-plated initial buckle on my belt that I had given my father the previous Christmas but borrowed to wear to California. After all, we had the same initial. When he wore it, it was always concealed by his vest.

At the Y, where I owed a week's rent, I left an IOU on the dresser, giving my address as Hereford, Texas. I then went down the fire escape to the second floor, where the last flight of stairs was suspended above the dark alley. I did not weigh enough, even with my suitcase, to lower the stairs to the ground. When I lowered and dropped my bag I was puzzled by the silence of its fall. I then let myself hang, my legs dangling, and let go, falling silently into a mound of fresh garbage. It stuck to my hands and clothes as I groped in it for my bag. I could smell it, all right, but I couldn't see it until I got into the light at the end of the alley. Smears of grease and gravy, salad greens, chunks of Jell-O, clung to my pants. I took a streetcar to Echo Lake Park, where I sat on the boat pier, my feet in the water, while I cleaned my socks and shoes.

The bus to Hereford, Texas, which proved to be near Amarillo, went through Phoenix and Globe, in Arizona, which were places I had missed on the trip west. The bus went through without stopping, but the drivers changed. I dozed off during the day, but I was usually awake most of the night. In a country with so much to see, it helped to see just a small piece of it under streetlights.

Without the high false fronts on the stores in Hereford I might have gone right through it and not seen it. The sunset burned like a fire in the second-floor windows of the general store. All around it, in every direction, the panhandle was as boundless and bare as the sea. Having seen the sea, I could say that. It even had the sort of dip and swell that the sea has. The man in the general store knew my Uncle Dwight, but there was no way to get in touch with him. His farm was about eight miles southeast, which was a long way to walk carrying a suitcase. But if I left the suitcase with him, I could walk it. He led me into the street, which was almost dark, but the sky was so full of light I blinked to look at it. He pointed out to me the trail I should follow, and the wire poles along it looked no higher than fence posts. The road was little more than smoothed-over grass, and once it got dark it would be hard to see it. What I had to look for, once it got dark, were the lights of his house and his tractor. He kept it going day and night. If I didn't see it, I would hear the cough of the engine. The light for me to keep my eye on, of course, was the one that stayed in one place. That was the house. If I walked at a good smart clip I could do it in about two hours.

After two days and two nights on the bus it felt good to walk. At one point, where I was on a rise, I could see the lights of Amarillo, like a cluster of stars. I could hear the tractor coughing before I saw it, and it sounded like a plug was missing. Some time later, when it made a turn, the lights came toward me like a locomotive. The last thing I saw was the feeble lampglow at a window of the house. I had never asked myself what he might have as a farm. A farm to me was a big old house, with some barns, and perhaps some trees along one side as a windbreak. What I saw slowly emerging in the milky darkness was a building no larger than my Uncle Harry's cobshed, set up on concrete blocks. A line of wash, like ghosts, hung to one side, where a machine of some sort was covered with a tarpaulin. Fifty or sixty yards away from the house were two sheds, and still further away was the peaked roof of a privy. The white spots in the yard were Leghorn chickens. Way, way off to the south, where the sky was darkest, the dim lights of the tractor flickered, and it made me so mournful and lonely I wanted to cry. If I had not come so far and was not so tired, I would have turned back. An eerie mauve and crimson afterglow filled the western horizon, like the earth was burning. Until I was right there in the yard, beside the sagging line of wash, the dog under the house neither saw nor heard me. When he came at me barking, he scared me out of my wits. I probably let out a yell. At the door to

171

the house, up three steps from the yard, a woman appeared with a clothes basket. She called off the dog, then said, "You're Wright?" I said that I was. "I'm Agnes," she said. "Dwight's on the tractor."

With the light behind her I could not see her face.

"Where's your bag?"

I explained that I had left it in Hereford, since I had to walk.

"Dwight's not going to like that," she said. "It means he's got to go fetch it." When I said nothing, she added, "I suppose you're hungry," and beckoned me to come in.

In the morning I saw nothing but the food on my plate, the slit of light at the window. It was on the horizon, but it might have been attached to the blind. Dawn. Sunrise would not come for another hour. The wind blowing under the house puffed dust between the floorboards, like smoke. There was never any talk. My Uncle would slip off his coveralls, like a flight suit, and eat in his two suits of underwear: one of fine, snug-fitting wool, flecked with gray, like a pigeon; the other of heavy, nubby cotton flannel with the elbows patched with quilting, the fly-seat yawning. The outer suit would come off in the spring, but the inner suit was part of my Uncle. I once saw him, plucked like a chicken, standing in a small wash basin of water while Agnes wiped him off with a damp towel. Dust. He was dusted rather than washed.*

Sometime before dawn, the wind rising, I was awakened by the cough of the tractor approaching the house. It

*Cause for Wonder, 1963.

went on coughing while I pulled on the clothes Agnes brought me—itchy underwear and socks, two heavy flannel shirts, coveralls still stiff from drying on the wash line, cold as ice.

Agnes had explained to me the night before that I would take over the tractor when Dwight brought it in in the morning, the engine never stopping because it was so hard to start. While I gulped hot biscuits and eggs fried in pork fat I could hear my uncle cursing. What was the trouble? It was just his way of keeping warm, talking to himself. When he came into the house dust caked his face, like the men I had seen in grain elevators. He did not look pleased when he saw me sitting there eating his food. He wore a cap with ear muffs, coveralls like mine, the legs tucked into three-buckle galoshes. I wouldn't know until Sunday what he really looked like, when I would first see him without his cap on—not because it was the Lord's day of rest, but my uncle's day off. His forehead, ears and neck were white as flour, the rest of his face was dark as an Indian's. Where had I seen him before? He could have been the brother of William S. Hart. He had the same steely, watery-blue eyes and thin-lipped mouth. When he smiled I could see the dirt caked at the roots of his teeth.

He didn't say who he was, or ask who I was, but came to the table and opened up a biscuit, smeared it in the pork fat, then put it in his mouth. I understood right then that you didn't talk to him while he was trying to eat. My uncle was a lean wiry man who just naturally stood with his legs flexed, as if he meant to hop. When he burned himself with a swallow of hot coffee he made a face just

173

like I would, with his eyes creased, then he let out a stream of curses. I followed him out in the yard, where the crack of dawn was right there on the horizon like a knife slit, then we carried between us a milk can full of kerosene to the John Deere tractor. It took both of us to lift it as high as the fuel tank, and pouring it into the funnel I got my gloves and hands soaked. He shouted at me, above the cough of the motor, if I knew how to steer a tractor? I nodded that I did. He rode along behind me, seated on one of the gang plows, letting his hand trail in the loam turned up by the plow blade. His section of land was about 1,800 acres, and I could see only a portion of it at one time. With the tractor running day and night it would take a month or more to get it plowed. On the west side, headed south, the wind in my face was so cold it made my eyes blur. Headed north, the dust raised by the plows blew over my head like a cloud of smoke. But when he saw I could manage the tractor on the turns he got off the plows and walked back toward the house, his arms raised from his sides as if he carried two pails. In that great empty expanse, the sun just rising, he looked like a bug and hardly seemed to move. When the light in the house turned off I missed it.

I'd been plowing half the morning before I noticed how the big jackrabbits moved just enough to stay clear of the plows. They would wait until the last second, then hop just enough to be clear of the blades. The whole section of land I was on had never before been turned by a plow. Only cattle had grazed it, most of them the white-faced Herefords that stood along the fence to watch me pass. I didn't know at that point that I was turning topsoil that had been centuries in the making. My uncle knew it, and it was why he had gambled on planting grain where it seldom rained. If it would grow grass, he argued, it would also grow wheat. Just five years before he had leased 1,200 acres, and he and Agnes, working alone, had harvested a crop worth more than $30,000. It hadn't rained a winter since then, but he was sure that it would.

In the sky around me, maybe twenty miles away, I could see cloud masses forming and drifting. I could even see mauve sheets of rain falling somewhere. A few days of steady rain was all that was needed, then months of hot sun. I thought I would die of hunger before I saw Agnes, followed by the dog, between the plowed land and the house. She brought me my lunch in a syrup pail, with a jar of black coffee. I'd never cared much for coffee, but I got to like it fine. The dog would stay with me, watching me eat, then he would trail in the fresh furrows left by the plows. When a rabbit moved, he tried to head it off and keep it running in the plowed section. He ran like the wind, so low to the ground that a plowed furrow would send him tumbling. It was hard to see the grass-colored rabbits when he chased them, just the crazy zig-zagging patterns made by the dog, like he was chasing flies. He was a sort of spitz, mixed with collie, his fur a mat of burrs picked up from the grass. His big stunt was to run straight at the Herefords if he found them all lined up like a wall at the fence. He would go right for them like a streak, and at the last split second they would break and panic, going off with their tails up, bellowing. We both loved it. I would stop the tractor and give him some attention. He was Agnes' dog. For one reason or another he didn't like Dwight. I think it was because Dwight would often shoot toward him when the two of them did

175

a little hunting. It was Dwight who gave him the name of
Jesus, because of the way a dead-looking rabbit would
spring to life when he saw him.

*Two hours before dawn we had left the dark house to
shoot at what I thought might be cattle rustlers. In the
windless pause before my Uncle ran forward hooting like
an Indian, I prepared myself to shoot it out with Billy the
Kid. When Dwight ran forward, hooting, I shot into the
air over his head. I heard a great flapping of wings, but
very little honking. I think I managed to fire two or three
times. Still dark, we came back to the house where Agnes
had coffee perking and a fire going. When the sky was
light we went out to see if we had bagged any birds. Just
shooting blind into the rising flock we had bagged nine.
So we had fresh gamy meat for two weeks and lead shot
on my plate in the evening, some of which I kept and
used over in a bee-bee gun.**

The John Deere tractor, until I got used to it, sounded
like a plug was missing and it was about to stop running.
It ran on the cheapest fuel, however, and once you got it
started it was hard to stop. To start it up, you had to give
the flywheel a spin, which scared the hell out of me because of the way it backfired. The first time it died on me
I couldn't get it restarted, and Dwight knew it right away
when the coughing stopped. He could hear that the way
he could hear a rise or fall in the wind. He had got out of
bed at about seven in the morning and walked the half
mile or so to where I was stalled. That gave me plenty of
time to watch him coming, his arms high from his sides

*Cause for Wonder.

like a winded chicken. He was so mad he hardly troubled to curse me, and grabbed the flywheel like he meant to tear it off. He didn't catch it just right, and the loud back-fire lifted him off his feet. That made him even madder, and less smart about it, and when he grabbed the wheel it spun him like a top and thumped him hard against one of the wheels. That hurt him so bad, and he was so ashamed, tears came to his eyes. If he had had a club big enough, or an axe, I think he would have chopped the John Deere to pieces. The reason he hated his father the way he did, as Winona had said, was that they were so much alike. They were both hard-driving, ambitious men who were accustomed to putting the harness on others as well as themselves. It almost killed him to have the trac-tor, right before my eyes, make a fool of him. It fright-ened me like the devil just to watch him, but when it was over I liked him better, and he was friendlier with me. By the time we got it started we were both so worn out we just got on it and rode it back to the house, where he went back to bed, and I sat in the sun where it warmed the wall. It made a difference between us, not such a big one that my job got to be any softer, but I had become a hired hand and he didn't have to watch me to know I was working.

As a rule I rode the tractor all day, and he rode it at night. He slept until early afternoon, then he did what needed doing around the place. Agnes raised chickens for the eggs we lived on, and the one she stewed or fried on Sunday. By afternoon the sun would heat up the house, but the way the wind blew around and beneath it, it would soon cool off in the evening. After supper we would sit around the range in the kitchen, with the oven door open. Agnes always had her mending to do, or washing, or the baking of bread she did on Mondays, and she was not a person who liked to talk while she worked. Nor had I ever before lived with a woman who didn't seem to like me. Not that she *dis*liked me, but at most she felt neutral. In the house she liked me to keep in my place. The year he made a lot of money Dwight had bought a big console radio in Kansas City that required a lot of batteries to run it. He got tired of trying to keep the batteries charged, so all it did was sit there with her sewing on it. In the space on the floor beneath there were two big cartons of Haldemann-Julius Little Blue Books. They sold for five cents each, and my uncle had bought two or three hundred of them. He was a great reader, over the winter, and read the books that he liked several times. Most of the books exposed religious hypocrisy and fakery. There were also books on geology, history and travel, so I didn't lack for something to read. I often carried one of these books in my pocket and read it when I stopped for lunch. What surprised me was how much my uncle loved to talk. On the day I had off we might sit up till almost midnight doing nothing but talking. A lot of what I said got him to laughing so hard his sides ached, and he could hardly stop. He loved to hear me talk about Pacific Union College, and the stuff they believed. I liked the way his eyes watered when he laughed, and the way they twinkled when he looked at me. The good talk we often had was no reason, however, I shouldn't be on the tractor at dawn the next morning.

That morning I heard the dawn crack like a whip. A little later I could peer out and see the wind where there was neither dust, lines of wash, nor even grass to blow. The yard was like a table, with a dull, flat gloss where the shoes buffed it toward the privy. Scoured by the wind, the cracks had been picked clean by the chickens. Out there, as nowhere else, I could see the wind. The five minutes in the morning I lay in a stupor listening to Agnes build the fire, I would face the window, the dawn like a slit at the base of a door. In the kitchen Agnes would put fresh cobs on the banked fire. Was it the sparks in the chimney, the crackle in the stove? The cats would hear it, five or six of them. With the first draw of the fire they would start from the grain sheds toward the house, a distance of about one hundred yards. Was that so far? It can be if you crawl. In the dawn light I would see only the white cats, or those that were spotted, moving toward the house like primitive or crippled reptiles. How explain it? The invisible thrust of the wind. The hard peltless yard gave them no hold. Even the chickens, a witless bird, had learned never to leave the shelter of the house at the risk of blowing away, like paper bags. A strip of chicken wire, like a net, had been stretched to the windward of the yard to catch them. They would stick like rags, or wads of cotton, till my Aunt would go out and pick them off. The cats and hens were quick to learn that the wind would prevail. My Aunt Agnes knew, but she preferred not to admit it. The last to learn was my Uncle Dwight.*

The way Agnes looked after my Uncle Dwight helped me to see why it was she seemed so neutral toward me. Dwight was hers. She liked him so much she didn't want to share him with anybody. The way he could talk

*Cause for Wonder.

pleased her, but the pleasure he showed when I talked made her frown and turn to her mending. She was not a pretty woman, her skin darkened by the weather, her hands like those of a man and chapped at the wrists, but I knew that she was a woman my uncle could take pride in. He had found her in Kansas, put her in a buggy and driven southwest till they came to the Pecos River in New Mexico. There he homesteaded a claim and raised sheep. Why didn't they have children? She would have liked kids of her own better than she liked me. Dwight was so independent in all of his thinking, he might not have wanted to share Agnes with them. He talked to her the way he did to me, but he considered me a better listener. I would come back at him. And he liked that. He said a lot of things just to rile me. I had also read some books that he hadn't, and that both pleased and shamed him. Sometimes he would put his hands to his face and just think about it for a moment, in silence.

My Uncle Dwight had not had, as he said, much schooling, preferring to educate himself by reading, but he talked in the assured manner of a man who could give a sermon. Words came to him easily, and quickly. His accent was like none I had heard, as if he had lived with strange people. I would hear nothing like it until I heard ballad singers on records. When he listened to me, his head tilted as if for a portrait, I felt in his gaze his admiration for his own kind. Was that what I was? Were we both pieces chipped from the same block? It pleased me to think that we might be, because I felt for him a secret admiration. He was strong. His mind was sharp as the glint of his eye. If the great men I had heard of were gathered together around a stalled tractor on the Texas panhandle, my uncle would prove to be the equal or the superior to most of them. They would listen in silence and admiration as he cursed.

On his homestead on the Pecos River, near Roswell, Dwight had found small six-sided rocks, with one or both ends sharpened to a point, like a pencil, around the holes of small rodents. They were locally known as Pecos diamonds. He kept a sampling of them in a Bull Durham tobacco sack, and brought them out to confound city hicks like me. What in the world had led God, he asked me, to make something like that in a hole in the ground? Nothing pleased him more than the foolishness of God compared to the almighty mysteries of nature.

The greatest marvel of nature on which he had set eyes were the Carlsbad Caverns in southern New Mexico. Dwight wanted me to see them the way Winona wanted me to see God. We stopped plowing for three days to drive there in his Willys Knight sedan, the car he kept under the tarpaulin beside the house. It still had the original tires on it, and the tools under the seat had never been used. A film of dust made it all one color, like his face when he came in from plowing. It pleased him to sit in the back seat with Agnes and let me drive. I knew about Willys Knights, and their sleeve-valve motors, from the one my father had had in Omaha that my Uncle Verne and I would take on long rides into Iowa and Kansas. On the curves I could look back and see the blue exhaust.

Jules Verne could have used the Carlsbad Caverns when he wrote *A Journey to the Center of the Earth.*

That's what the caverns were like. We went down there with a large group of people who had come from places as far as Minneapolis and Chicago. We all gathered in a huge cavernous room, near a large rock, and sang the hymn "Rock of Ages." When our names were called out we would reply where we had come from. Learning I was from Chicago, a man from Milwaukee came to me and threw his arms around me. He had lived in Chicago, and often visited Lincoln Park.

I found the caverns as fantastic as my uncle had said but not so mystifying as the Pecos diamonds. At first I figured Indians must have made them and these little rodents ran off with them. But why would an Indian spend his life doing something like that? On our way back to Hereford we made a detour to see what was left, if anything, of their homestead. The shack was still there, the color of rusted machinery, and there were signs that some bums or prospectors had lived in it. I didn't see much that sheep could have grazed on, but along the rimrock of the Pecos River we found a lot of holes made by rodents, and some with these little rocks around them. They were similar, but whoever made them got tired and quit before they were finished, leaving only one end of the rock pointed. It wasn't like a smart Indian to start something, and work hard at it, then leave it unfinished.

In an alley in Clovis—I forget why I was there—I stepped on a nail that went right through the sole of my shoe. Agnes had never shown any interest in me until I stepped on that nail. Back in Hereford the first thing she did was heat a kettle of water for me to soak my foot in. Until the soreness was gone she didn't think I should work all day on the tractor, and I agreed. Actually, until we took the trip, I had more or less forgotten how close we were to the desert. The one thing you could say for sure about a desert was that it seldom rained. The idea that it wasn't going to rain in Hereford proved to be one that I couldn't get rid of. The more I looked around, in every direction, the drier it looked. What was I doing? I was working like a horse for thirty dollars a month and board that was giving me the hives. That was what Agnes told me when I began to scratch. Hives came from eating nothing much but eggs fried in pork fat, and biscuits.

My uncle got his pork and fat from a family eighteen miles to the east that raised hogs and horses. Their name was Gudger. The big house they lived in and the barns around it had once been part of a ranch, but the over-grazed land was no longer useful to cattle. From four or five miles away I could see the branches of a dead tree, the bleached color of bones, sticking up from the plain like antlers. There wasn't a leaf on it, the bark was peeled off, and the house and the barns were the same weathered color. The Gudger business in horses had fallen off, but they hobbled the few they had left and let them wander around. There were kids in the yard when we drove up, the smaller ones with hair that made them look like goblins. They were busy carrying buckets of hot water to a mound in the yard, under a branch of the tree. In the mound was a big wooden vat, wide and deep enough to dip a hog into. The hog my uncle had agreed to buy a part of was in a fenced-in area beside the barn. He was so big that from the rear he looked like the mound of earth over a storm cave. I had to stoop over to see his feet, no bigger than the bungs you use to plug up a barrel. I couldn't believe that anything so gross had such delicate feet. Set into his huge face, like buttons, were his little eyes and long silvery lashes. He didn't mind at all my patting his back like the rump of a horse.

On our ride to the Gudgers' I had sat in the car with Dwight's Winchester rifle across my lap. On windless days I might take it along on the tractor and take potshots at a few rabbits. In a landscape so big and empty it was hard to judge how far away I was from a rabbit. My rifle bullets would kick up the dirt maybe twenty yards in front of them. I could see the arc of the bullet as it left the barrel. The older, smarter jacks would hop off a little ways, then sit up like penguins and watch me. So far as I know, I never hit one of them.

Dwight had explained to me how to shoot a hog. You take an ear of corn, with the tassels still on it, and stick the smaller end in your open fly. The hog either sees the ear of corn or he sniffs it, and comes slowly waddling toward you. When he's about a gun-barrel length away you aim right between his eyes and pull the trigger. He's so surprised, he doesn't know what hit him. The only thing that's changed is the little black hole between his eyes. He might just stand there, propped like a barrel, until you take a fence post and tilt him over. It might take two or three people to budge him. Then the one with the butcher knife slits his throat and catches the blood in the pan while his heart is still pumping. It's the blood that makes the best sausage anybody ever ate.

It never crossed my mind, listening to what he told me, that I would be the one to shoot the hog. I walked along

184

beside him to the split rail fence, where he reached into the pen for a tasseled ear of corn. "Here you are, kid," he said, handing it to me, then he held the gun while I loosened the buttons and stuck it in my fly. I didn't have the time to think as to whether I wanted to do it, before it was done. I climbed over the fence about ten yards to his left, and Dwight handed me the rifle, after he'd cocked it. There was just the three of us, my Uncle Dwight, me and the hog. The hog lumbered toward me, just the way Dwight had said, then he stopped and raised his big head to look at the corn. I had never before been so close to anything so big. I could see the long silvery lashes to his eyes. He wasn't fierce at all, just huge, making little grunts like a sow with a litter, his ears alone so big and furry they didn't look real. He gave me all the time in the world to aim, and he came in so close I could have reached out and touched him. Right between his eyes I saw the hole I had made, but I hadn't heard a sound. The two of us just stood there facing each other, like Dwight had in mind taking our picture, only he was quick to scramble over the fence and slide a post under the hog's belly. When he felt that post give him a prod, he spread his legs a little bit, which propped him like a barrel. Dwight yelled at me to give him a hand, and I put down the gun and tried to help him. The hog didn't budge. Three or four of the kids who had heard the gunshot scrambled over the fence and helped us push on him. We managed to rock him over, and with his feet in the air he gave a mighty shudder, stiffening his legs. The rest of it went just the way Dwight had described it, the blood pumping from his throat as black as oil, and before the

185

gate to the fence was lowered Mr. Gudger was there with a team of horses. It took some hauling to drag him over to the tree, get the rope through the pulley and truss him up. Trussed up like that, hung out his full length, he looked more like an ox than a hog. The idea was to let him soak for a bit in the hot water, then hoist him out so all the little Gudgers could scrape at his hide with knives and pieces of broken glass. They were expert at it, and with the bristles shaved off he was almost pink. The first part of him to go was the head, which they propped in a big bucket, and in no more time than it took me to blink it was covered with flies. Every time something was added to the pail the flies rose in a cloud, buzzing like hornets. The smell of the wet hog, the sight of the steaming guts, the way the flies rose up in a cloud, then settled, led me to sort of stand off to one side watching, but I soon felt so woozy I had to lean on the car. Every time I looked at the hog he was smaller, as Mr. Gudger and my uncle hacked away at him. Soon there was nothing much but just the huge pair of hams, turning slowly as the wind blew on them, the whole pack of little Gudgers running beneath like yapping dogs.

We were all called to the house by Mrs. Gudger to eat the pies she had baked, and drink coffee. There were no rugs in the house, just the plank floor that the dust puffed through when the wind blew. We sat at a table in the kitchen, and when I raised my eyes I could see the sky through the chinks in the shingles. It rained so little they didn't have to worry about it raining inside. If I had seen that when I first arrived I might have had second thoughts about working for my uncle, but I would have missed seeing the Carlsbad Caverns, the Pecos diamonds, and the hog I shot with my uncle watching. I liked that most of all, since he would have liked nothing better than to see me miss.

Mrs. Gudger, a worn, stooped old woman with a flour-white face, but her hair black as a stove lid, gave me a piece of her pie to take along with me, I liked it so much. She did the baking, but her oldest daughter, Georgia, did the cooking. Georgia wore a short-sleeved shirt and a pair of khaki work pants with the legs cut off at the knees. She had taffy-colored hair, like her brothers, and a light brown tan all over. Dwight caught me looking at her. But who wouldn't look at a girl as old as she was wearing knee pants instead of a skirt? From the way she liked to ride horses, bareback, she had a shine between her legs, like leather, and I had seen so many girls in the last few months I was glad I didn't have to choose one of them.

As the boy had never looked upon the sea, nor any body of water he couldn't see over, he had no word for the landscape that he faced. The land itself seemed to roll like the floors in amusement parks. Without seeming to climb they would be on a rise with the earth gliding away before them, and in the faraway hollow there were towns a day's ride away. The wheels turned, the earth seemed to flow beneath the buggy, like dirty water, but nothing else changed and they seemed to be standing still. Here and there white-faced cattle, known as Herefords, stood in rows along the barbed wire fence as if they had never seen a buggy, a horse, or a small boy before. They were always still there, as if painted on the fence when he turned and looked. Then the road itself came to an end and they followed the wavering lines in the grass that the wheels had made the week before, on their way out. And when they came within sight of the farm—it seemed to recede, and they seemed to stalk it—the boy knew that he was nearing the rim of the world. What would he see when he peered over it? The hog. The hog would prove to be part of it. But the bleak house, with the boarded windows, was like a caboose left on a siding, and behind this house the world seemed to end. In the yard was a tree, but it would be wrong to say that the house and the tree stood on the sky, or that the body of the hog, small as it appeared, was dwarfed by it. It swung from the tree like some strange bellied fruit. Swarming about in the yard were large boys with knives, sharpened pieces of metal, and small boys with long spears of broken glass. They all attacked the hog, hooting like Indians, and used whatever they had in hand to shave the stiff red bristles from the hog's hide. The boy could see a small hole, like a third eye, in the center of the hog's dripping head. The mouth was curved in a smile as if the swarm of boys scraping his hide tickled him. . . . From one of the blood-smeared pails in the yard a black cloud of flies rose into the air, then settled again. They made a sound as if the roaring wind had been siphoned into a bottle, leaving the yard empty and the flies trapped inside . . . pelting the sides like a quick summer rain. *

By the first week of April it still hadn't rained. I began to think, while I was on the tractor, how great it was in

* "The Rites of Spring," 1952.

April in Lincoln Park, with the grass greening and the trees leafing. Along with everything else I liked, it would rain. Even on Larrabee Street I liked the way it smelled after a rain. Some of these days I could see it was raining somewhere, but Texas was just too big for it to rain all over. That would be true with or without Georgia Gudger. Another problem was that she didn't know better, and I did.

With all day on the tractor to think about the future, it seemed drier and drier to me in the present. All the money I would get, if and when it rained, seemed to mean less to me than a week or two in Chicago with my friends. It would take me that long to tell them about my adventures, and my plan to go to Pomona College. I hoped to persuade Maurie Johnson, whose father had sold his dairy to Bordens, to go along with me. He would have the money. His father had bought an interest in a North Side bank. I had all but forgotten that Maurie had told me I might get a job in the bank over the summer. Working in a bank appealed to me more than a ten-hour day on a tractor.

The thinking I did about the future led my mind to wander while I was on the tractor. I got the plows out of line, and trying to get them straight, one of them jammed in the sod and stalled the engine. I knew my uncle would soon miss the racket of the tractor, and it made me a little frantic. I just about skinned my palms trying to spin the flywheel, but she wouldn't catch. When I looked back toward the house there was Dwight, with the dog, Jesus, coming toward me. To be caught like that and humiliated was one of the worst things that had happened to me. It seemed forever before he reached me, the dog running on

189

ahead to scare up rabbits, and I could see the way he was cursing from the way his head pumped, like he was gagging. I would have heard it all before, but I had no choice but to listen to it. But what I also needed the most at that moment was an excuse to quit, and he had given it to me. While he had his back to me, wrestling with the flywheel, I just walked off. It was such a big and risky decision my throat ached, and I almost bawled. I'd gone about two hundred yards before he yelled at me, but I didn't look back. He called my name—"Wright!" he hollered. "Oh, Wright!"—which was almost as strange as hearing my father call me "son," and filled my eyes with tears. I had my fists doubled up so hard my fingers hurt. Before I reached the house he had the tractor started and I could hear the cough blowing on the wind, but he stayed out there, plowing up the section, and was out of my sight when I glanced back.

Agnes was hanging out her wash at the side of the house while I packed my bag. I would have taken off with it, and headed for Hereford, but the only money I had was what Dwight owed me. Having to drive me into Hereford would be another thing he had against me. Agnes didn't question me as to what had happened, or where it was I thought I was going, and toward three o'clock, because he was getting hungry, Dwight came in with the tractor. When he saw my packed bag he knew what I was up to. He had to get back at me, so he said, "If you're dam-fool enough to throw away ten thousand dollars it's better I know it now than later."

First of all, it was more like seven thousand, and the problem was that I wasn't dam-fool enough. In just

190

walking out on him the way I was doing I had an advantage that he didn't know how to handle. He changed his clothes, which was a lot of trouble, just to drive me into Hereford. There was a train at five o'clock that would take me to Amarillo, where I would catch the night train to Chicago. He gave me forty dollars cash, which would cover my fare, then a twenty-dollar check on an Amarillo bank I figured might bounce. The only checks I knew about, my father's, weren't worth the paper they were written on.

We got to Hereford about two hours too early, where my uncle worked up a great story as to how I was called back to Chicago on an emergency. It was not unusual for something to get to me, like the problems I got into at Pacific Union College, but I knew it was unusual for something like me to get to my Uncle Dwight. Because his pride was bigger than mine, it hurt him worse. Mad as it made him, I could also see that it had increased his respect for me. The look he gave me was that he knew we were one of a kind. We just sat there in the store, our feet on the stoveboard, sharing the package of gingersnaps he had bought me, and by the time the local train had come over from Clovis things were pretty normal between us. I really liked him, as big a fool as I thought him to be.

*A*s I rode north on the Clark streetcar from the Loop,
I could look up ahead to the green of Lincoln Park,
or down the narrow streets to the east to the trees along
the bridle path and the lake and the sky like the rim of
the world. I didn't like everything I saw, but it was home.
My father was still in bed, a can of Carnation milk on
the windowsill, with green around the holes punched in
the can. In the warm spring drizzle I walked over to Ogden Avenue, and south to the Larrabee Y. They had a
stocky ex-wrestler working in the lobby with a bandage
on his forehead where someone had hit him with a cue
ball. The stairs to the locker room still had the smell of
pool chlorine, but the locker room itself had the sweet
smell of cheap perfume. That's how fast things can
change when your back is turned.

I took a room at the back of the Y, where I could hear the balls bounce, then I looked up my old high school friends and told them all about Texas and Pomona College. What I found was that you can't explain some things to people who have always lived in Chicago. They all had families to tie them down, and I didn't. They all knew what they were going to do, and I didn't. On Saturday nights, after we had been to a movie, I might spend the night with Maurie Johnson or Bill Miller. There were eight people in the Miller family so it was easy to make room for me at their table. In the last few years Mrs. Miller had grown so large a place had been made for her in the basement, off the kitchen, so she wouldn't have to use the stairs. Mr. Miller had bought a Hupmobile sedan, which he paid us fifty cents an hour to wax. On Sundays he parked it in the front yard so the water he used to wash it wouldn't be wasted.

Across the street from the Millers the older Baker girl had a boyfriend who went to Northwestern. On the weekends they would sit in his Scripps Booth roadster, the red and green gems glowing in the dashboard light. The Baker girl had a younger sister, Lois, who first had to help her mother with the dishes before she could come out and sit on the porch steps, hugging her knees. Her father sat there after supper in his B.V.D.'s, hosing the trees so the water would drip on the grass and the walk. If her sister's boyfriend didn't come down from Northwestern, she might ask us all over to stir some fudge or sing along with her at the piano. We harmonized pretty good "How Deep Is the Ocean," "Button up Your Overcoat" and "Little White Lies." The one that suited my voice the best was "Little White Lies."

Lois wasn't old enough as yet to have real boyfriends, but not many of the boys knew it. With her long flat feet in tennis sneakers, she was still about half an inch taller than I was. Her favorite color at the time was sky-blue-pink. Since she was not yet in her first year of high school she didn't have the interest in college that I did. I was able to help her with her charcoal drawing and the problems she was having raising Belgian hares. Some of them were mean. The male Belgian hare would eat his own litter if you didn't watch him. Lois would sit with one of the big ones in her lap while I told her about butchering the hog in Texas, or the flood I escaped from in Mississippi. Almost anything I said made her laugh like she was being tickled. The way I stared at her night after night, it's hard to explain why what I see the clearest is the back of her neck. The barber she went to always used the clippers, which was one thing that drove her crazy. She looked forward to wearing her hair in braids that hung down to her waist.

Mrs. Baker welcomed my help with the dishes, and might invite me to go to a movie with them. I was with Lois, sitting down near the front, when we saw *All Quiet on the Western Front*, and she almost died. Mrs. Baker liked me, and it worried her to think what Lois would do while I was off in California. Already the boys her older sister brought home asked for Lois the next time they called. She was only fourteen, but none of them seemed to mind. If I planned to spend four years in California, with just June, July and August in Chicago, Mrs. Baker could feel in her bones that we were all in for a lot of surprises.

After my work at the Y, I would take the streetcar and ride the thirty minutes north to the Baker house. If Lois wasn't in the hammock on the porch, she would be in her room at the back of the house, listening to Wayne King at the Aragon. I would come in from the alley, passing her hutch of Belgian hares, and climb the posts of the screened-in porch to the roof. The screen to her window was unlatched, and I could either crawl in or she could crawl out and sit there with me. Right down the hall were her two bratty little brothers, with her older sister right next to the bathroom. For an older sister she was exceptionally broad-minded. Mr. and Mrs. Baker had the bedroom at the front where I could often hear the radio playing. I could tell from the glances Mrs. Baker often gave me that she knew pretty well what we were up to. At the time I was less informed than she was. Until I got to college, and read about it somewhere, I didn't know that what we had been up to was "bundling." The early settlers used to do it. Not knowing what it was, I didn't enjoy it as much as I might have. Mrs. Baker believed that there was nothing in the world Lois would remember longer than what she was now doing and feeling. Lois about died every time she heard that, but she believed it was the truth.

The friend I talked to the most, besides Lois and her mother, was a boy at the Y named Laurie Lusk. Laurie played right tackle for Lane Tech, and he was interested in going on to college. On his graduation his father gave him a Model A Ford touring, with yellow wire wheels and a new set of Kelly Springfield tires. It was Laurie's idea, as much as it was mine, that we would drive it all the way to California, the two of us camping out and sharing the expenses. Yet if I hadn't talked so much about Pomona College, and what the winter was like in California, I might have found some excuse to stay in Chicago rather than say goodbye to Lois Baker, which took me almost a week.

And yet I hardly remember our actually leaving. It was Mrs. Baker who did most of the crying, with Lois' little brother Charlie being the biggest nuisance. I don't remember how it was with Maurie Johnson, or Bill Miller, or all my friends at the Y, or what I said to my father, or he said to me. I was so anxious to get away before something went wrong I didn't write my Aunt Winona about it, fearing that might jinx it, and I forgot the racing goggles I had bought for driving in the sun and wind with the top down. I don't remember the route we took out of Chicago, or where it was we crossed the Mississippi, or if we stopped, as we had planned, in Shenandoah, Iowa, where Shelley had gone and learned to play horseshoes, but we did get eaten up by mosquitoes the night we slept in the car near Des Moines.

In Omaha the grass was all chewed up in front of the Mulligan house. Mr. Mulligan was asleep, still being a pressman, and Mrs. Mulligan didn't feel she should wake him, but she telephoned Joey at the *Daily News*, where he worked in the pressroom during the daytime. He got excited when he saw me, just the way he used to, his scalp glowing pink beneath his short blond hair. I could tell he resented the idea of Laurie now being my best friend. It was hard for us to talk, with the presses running, but I learned he had played football for Omaha

Tech and he was now engaged to Lillian Kovack, the pretty Polish girl whose hand I had held in the basement of the house when we played "Run Sheep Run." She had changed so much he wasn't sure at all I would recognize her, and worked as a clerk in McCrory's dime store. He didn't understand anybody as old and smart as I was wanting to go to school instead of working and getting married, especially so far away.

If we went through my hometown in Nebraska, and we pretty well had to, since it was on the Lincoln Highway, I don't remember anything about it. I may have been dozing while Laurie was driving, or I may have been thinking of California, or of college, or of making up my mind if we should head for Texas, just to see if it had rained on my uncle's farm near Hereford, or go straight through to Salt Lake via Wyoming, which was what we did. I don't remember too much about Salt Lake City either, except for the mountain water running along in the ditches, but somewhere along the way we did let the top down and were soon sunburned so bad we couldn't sleep. I do remember Needles, which was hot as fire, and I wanted to look around for the Big Six Studebaker my father and me and Don had left in a place called Siberia, but they had improved the road across that part of the desert and places like Siberia were no longer on it.

Nor was California, in September, much like the way I had described it to Laurie, the glare of light off the desert so strong we had to squint to see the hazy mountains. It wasn't the time for oranges, but in the shade of the trees we could see the way the groves swept back to the foot-

197

hills, which would be mountains back where we had come from. I was looking up ahead so hard for the college that we drove right by it, and had to come back. On one side was the desert, the air like ripples in glass, except where they had sprinklers running on a golf course, and on the other this dark green oasis. I wanted to arrive the way I had the first time, coming up from the Pacific Electric station with the eucalyptus trees framing a view of the mountains. On the campus they had the sprinklers running, and at that time in the morning, with the mist rising, it was like a Maxfield Parrish painting. We didn't see any students, just the ivy on the buildings and the blackbirds with their hatpin eyes. We drove up to the foothills just to look back at it, then we came back slow to where we could read what was engraved on the college gates—INCIPIT VITA NOVA—which I explained to Laurie meant "Here begins a new life." That was how I felt about it, and I had come to believe, thanks to some people I had met, that what you feel strongly enough about might happen. I was twenty years of age, and my Uncle Dwight would say it was about time.

Coda

*I*n my third year at Pomona College, about to leave for a *Wanderjahr* in Europe, I had a long talk with a girl who believed that boys had all the luck. She could not hitchhike, as I could, to Chicago, nor take a freighter to Greece, nor swim the Hellespont, nor live in an attic in Paris, nor see the world through a porthole. I shared her sense of injustice, but it did not lead me to question my good fortune. As a boy, I was at ease in the prevailing order. Who was I to change it? Surely Mother Nature, over the centuries, had given the matter considerable thought and worked it out the way we found it. If it was puzzling, and indeed it was, why nature favored some and not others, it nevertheless seemed natural that she should smile on a white Anglo-Saxon Protestant ignorant boy like me. Years later, recalling my friend's face, the way her eyes avoided mine on parting, I sensed that her smile had seamlessly mingled womanly pity and contempt. I had been so stitched and tailored to the prevailing mode I was at ease with her second-class status, contributing, as it did, to all the good things that were reserved for men.

My considerable experience of the world had not as yet inspired me to try to change it, nor did the way I perceived it depress or disturb me. I accepted things as I found them. If one day I proved to be deserving, I firmly believed I would be rewarded. I had this assurance, below the level of discussion, from all those people who had reared and shaped me, their feet on the ground, even as their eyes were set on the wild blue yonder.

The wild blue yonder of my imagination had not as yet been corrupted by an idea, nor had my spirit been dampered by disenchantment. I daily renewed my great expectations experienced in the words and music of popular songs. The optimism of Dixie, the nostalgia of the blues, charged the air I breathed with a shared intoxication, whether I looked to the past or the future. I could feel this about me like the hum of a powerhouse, or the tingling silence of a city at night, my gaze held by the lights on the rising span of a drawbridge. The *Rhapsody in Blue* confirmed what I was feeling, affirmed what I knew. If growing up meant to abandon these sentiments, Will's boy would be slow to grow up.